T0019851

Endorsements

Through heartbreaking, true stories of loss, *God Is Always with You* reminds us each day that, through godly counsel, the Bible, and prayer, we have access to a divine grace that can sustain us even in our darkest hour. A great resource for anyone who has experienced loss and anyone comforting grieving people.

Matthew S. Stanford, PhD | CEO, Hope and Healing Center & Institute; Author, *Madness & Grace: A Practical Guide for Pastoral Care and Serious Mental Illness*

Where do you find comfort when your soul has been shattered? When sorrow has splintered your soul, how do you face another day...hour...minute? If you are in a season of pain and anguish, you will find comfort and hope in these pages. Stories provide a lifeline; they connect us, anchor us, and provide us with the oxygen needed to endure. Without question, you will find the solace your soul is longing for right here and right now.

Colleen Swindoll-Thompson | Founder, Reframing Ministries at Insight for Living

No human being is immune to suffering. In the midst, it's common to ask *why?* or feel alone and cut off. The stories in this devotional are a light in darkness, illuminated personally by those who have walked along similar pathways. They are not fiction but wisdom gained from real, intense suffering that illustrate a common theme: sufferers are *never* alone. A God who *knows all* and understands purposes humans will never fully comprehend *is near*. The team at LifeSupport delivers impactful stories gleaned from hundreds of interviews. Each day, this devotional brings voices of encouragement to those just beginning or in the midst of their own pilgrimages. Daily, readers can experience powerful ways a God who himself suffered, died, and rose again reveals himself to those he loves.

Glen Bloomstrom | Chaplain (Colonel) US Army, retired; Director, Faith Community Engagement, LivingWorks Education

.   .

I remember the night vividly. Sitting on my deck one warm May evening with tears streaming down my face. I'm a "successful" surgeon whose marriage is failing. I was told as a new Christian that divorce is not an option, yet I knew this misery I was living in was no option for me or my son. I called my newfound friend and spiritual mentor, a man of God who once carried guns, was hooked on drugs, and controlled blocks of a city through violence and fear. Through my tears, I choked out my question: "I'm sorry to bother you. I've never been shot, stabbed, or in prison like you. But could I ask you about my marriage?" His response was short and revealing. "Tom, pain is pain. Jesus is the doctor you need." As shown in the piercing stories of this book, brutal pain is real. But even more real is our *true healer Christ*, who will wipe away every tear.

Tom Blee, MD | Trauma and Acute Care Surgeon; President and CEO, LIFEteam; Author, *How to Save a Surgeon: Stories of Impossible Healing*

God Is Always with You

31 Days of Hope and
Healing for Grief and Loss

BY THE TEAM AT LIFESUPPORT RESOURCES

BroadStreet
PUBLISHING

BroadStreet Publishing® Group, LLC
Savage, Minnesota, USA
BroadStreetPublishing.com

God Is Always with You: 31 Days of Hope and Healing for Grief and Loss
Copyright © 2022 5 Stone Media Group

978-1-4245-6418-7 (hardcover)
978-1-4245-6419-4 (e-book)

This book is not intended as a substitute for the medical advice of licensed therapists or physicians. These stories are intended to give comfort to those experiencing grief and loss. You should regularly consult a medical professional in matters relating to your mental and physical health needs.

All rights reserved. No part of this book may be reproduced in any form, except for brief quotations in printed reviews, without permission in writing from the publisher.

Scripture quotations marked NLT are taken from the Holy Bible, New Living Translation, copyright © 1996, 2004, 2015 by Tyndale House Foundation. Used by permission of Tyndale House Publishers, a Division of Tyndale House Ministries, Carol Stream, Illinois 60188. All rights reserved. Scripture quotations marked NIV are taken from The Holy Bible, New International Version® NIV®. Copyright © 1973, 1978, 1984, 2011 by Biblica, Inc.™ Used by permission. All rights reserved worldwide. Scripture quotations marked NASB are taken from the New American Standard Bible® (NASB), Copyright © 1960, 1962, 1963, 1968, 1971, 1972, 1973, 1975, 1977, 1995, 2020 by The Lockman Foundation. Used by permission. www.Lockman.org. Scripture quotations marked GW are taken from GOD'S WORD®, © 1995 God's Word to the Nations. Used by permission of God's Word Mission Society.

Stock or custom editions of BroadStreet Publishing titles may be purchased in bulk for educational, business, ministry, fundraising, or sales promotional use. For information, please email orders@broadstreetpublishing.com.

Cover and interior by Garborg Design Works | garborgdesign.com

Printed in China

22 23 24 25 26 5 4 3 2 1

Dedication

This devotional is dedicated to the survivors who generously shared the stories we tell, to the families of those survivors, and to the team of pastors and mental health professionals who advise us.

Contents

Introduction

As creators of LifeSupport resources for ministry and the LifeSupport podcast, we've had the opportunity to meet and interview dozens of generous survivors who have given us permission to use their stories to help others. These stories illustrate the truth that grief is a universal emotion and that the life of every Christian will include suffering. The idea that someone will be protected from harm because they are a Christian or simply because they pray hard enough is a myth.

God Is Always with You: 31 Days of Hope and Healing for Grief and Loss brings you stories of grief, organized by topic, which share the experiences of real people who have walked through the darkness of loss. Each daily story concludes with wise counsel and biblical insight from mental health professionals and pastors.

If you are in grief today or know someone who is, we have compiled this devotional for you. We hope that you might recognize your own struggle in these pages. We are praying that you will understand that you are not alone in your suffering and that you will find hope and healing as you discover a new way to walk through your pain.

Caution! This devotional contains stories of real people in pain and suffering that may trigger or intensify your own feelings. Finding a path through grief requires support from others. We encourage you to reach out to a local mental health professional or church for care.

Section 1

LOSS OF A SPOUSE

Day 1

NO FAIRY-TALE ENDING

Julie was living her fairy-tale life. She fell in love and married a man with a big smile and a bigger heart. He was a godly man, and he was her best friend. Ken was also handsome and healthy. He was a long-distance runner and was serious about exercise, one of the many things that attracted Julie to him.

When she married Ken, he had two teenage children. Two years later, Ken and Julie welcomed their son, Sam, into their family. Julie's husband and her kids were her world, and she could not ask for a better life. Every morning she would wake up and go to the kitchen to have her coffee. Sometimes she would just look out the window and think to herself, *This is all I've ever wanted. This is so amazing.*

Smiles, laughter, hugs, and kisses were a daily part of her life. Julie was young and lived in a protective bubble. She felt safe, secure, and loved. That protective bubble was shattered when Julie found out that her husband was diagnosed with a rare form of lung cancer. By the time Ken was diagnosed, the cancer was already in Stage 4. She was devastated. She wanted Ken to live, and she would do whatever it took.

Julie and her family traveled the country to find help, whether it was a clinical trial or a new miracle drug. They spent the next eighteen months doing whatever they could in hopes of a miracle. Julie truly believed that her husband would be a miracle and that he would have an incredible story to tell after he recovered. However, when they went to the clinical trials, they were turned away. They were told to just go home and be together while they could.

Ken helped Julie discover the power of her own faith because, through his sickness, Ken demonstrated the strength of his faith. He had experienced redemption in Christ years earlier, and his belief fed Julie's faith throughout the experiences of Ken's sickness and eventual death. Julie went to God because she had nothing else to go to that could save her or make her feel any better. Julie simply went to her knees and said, "I can't do this. If you want me to keep doing this or doing life, I need you, and you have to show up. I can't do this."

After the eighteen months, the obvious became apparent. Julie kept praying but also had to plan a funeral. Now she finally knew what utter despair and helplessness felt like for the first time in her life.

Ken passed away, and a new, completely different life was in store for Julie, one that she could never have imagined. She was now a widow with three children, and every day was a challenge to navigate, mentally, emotionally, and physically. She experienced different stages of grief, including anger, denial, bargaining, and depression.

Grief seemed like an enemy. However, over time, Julie learned that grief was not something she should fight. Grief was the cost of loving someone who died. It was the cost of living in a fallen world where people die, dreams die, fairness dies, and hope dies. But that brought God's love out in a bigger way for Julie.

Although she was a Christian and had been active in church, she now was experiencing God's love in a much different and more profound way. For Julie, her grief and trauma strengthened her relationship with God and strengthened her spiritually. Even though she couldn't see it early on after Ken died, she soon realized God was grooming her for the next step in her life.

Julie would go on to become a therapist and have her own practice. She also became a hospital chaplain. She now considers it an honor to walk alongside people in deep and dark loss and sorrow. She now uses her story, full of pain and suffering, to show others the power of God and how he was able to help her become an anchor for others who are trying to navigate through their own grief and trauma.

Wise Counsel and Biblical Insight

Allow God to Work in You in Times of Trauma

Christian counselor Tom Colbert says when we become vulnerable during our times of grief, only then can real changes be made in our lives. "If we're really going to have Christ come into our lives, we have to have a level of vulnerability," Colbert says. "And that is a really scary thing to people of trauma. But if you create that arena of respect where it's okay...because someone knows me, someone understands me. Someone has accepted me where I am. And it takes away from being labeled. There's no label anymore. It's not you. *You're not a personification of your trauma; you're a person.* And then, amazing things can happen."

God Uses Our Grief and Pain

Julie went through a very dark time after her husband passed away. She experienced tremendous pain, suffering, and grief. However, looking back now, she can now see that God used Ken's faith, even his sickness and death to draw her closer to him. She can now see God's true love and beauty in a world full of sickness, disease, and death. Julie now uses that experience and knowledge to help others who are suffering to see that same love from God she experienced.

God Is Bound to Us

"Who shall separate us from the love of Christ? Shall trouble or hardship or persecution or famine or nakedness or danger or sword?" (Romans 8:35 NIV).

PRAYER

Dear Lord, I am grieving the loss of a loved one, and this world now seems so dark, lonely, and lifeless. I know you do not want me to live this way and think these things. Please show me your light of love that I desperately need right now. Amen.

Day 2

WHY, GOD?

Cindy and her husband, Jerry, had a unique marriage, and she was just fine with that. They met when Cindy worked at an elementary school and Jerry was a deputy sheriff with the county. He would visit the school for its Drug Abuse Resistance Education (D.A.R.E.) program. They had a fun romance. Cindy had three daughters, and Jerry had no children of his own. They got married, and Jerry treated her daughters like his own. He was a great stepfather. Since Jerry worked in law enforcement, there were times Cindy would go on ride-alongs with him. It was a unique time together that they both enjoyed. Being married to a police officer was a journey for Cindy and her family, but they loved it.

Cindy eventually left her job at the elementary school, and she soon became a staff member at the family's church and oversaw the church's addiction recovery ministry. Jerry also volunteered his time to that ministry.

Jerry had seen many things during his time in law enforcement. He had experienced some traumatic things in the field, and over time, that started to take a toll on him mentally. He was diagnosed with PTSD and depression.

One day, Cindy and Jerry were driving to one of their daughter's houses to see their grandchildren when they were in a head-on collision. Cindy was in worse physical shape than Jerry, but after they recovered from their injuries, it became clear that the accident had more seriously affected Jerry's mental health. He became a different person; he was haunted by visions of the crash and by other scenes he had witnessed over the years as a deputy. Cindy and Jerry loved their hometown, but after the accident, Jerry felt they would have to move somewhere new. Everywhere he went he would replay horrible memories over and over. When Cindy and her family would drive somewhere, Jerry would have them take a different route to avoid the scene of the accident. Other times, he would express that he could not get the sights and sounds of the accident out of his head. He would just put his hands on his head and say, "What's going on in my head? I don't understand. Something's not right. It's getting worse, and I can't understand why this is happening to me."

Cindy knew she needed to do something to help her husband. She reached out to a couple of treatment facilities. However, since Jerry never abused substances, they turned him away. Jerry was getting sicker and more tormented. Cindy found that he had searched "suicide and your salvation" on his phone. She confronted him about it, but he denied that he had suicidal thoughts.

Cindy and her brother got together to remove all the guns from their home. She now knew that her husband wanted to kill himself, which caused a sickening feeling in her. She got so scared that she reached out to Jerry's sergeant. He came over to talk to Jerry and decided he needed to go to the hospital. Jerry was admitted for treatment, but once he was released, things continued to get worse.

One morning, Cindy left to go to the chiropractor, and Jerry stayed home. When she returned, she noticed that Jerry wasn't home, and her heart sank. She couldn't find him anywhere. Her brother came over and looked around the house, but he had no luck either. Her brother decided to look along a trail in the woods near their home, and that's where they found Jerry. He had taken his own life.

Cindy and Jerry had been married for twenty years. She never in her wildest dreams could imagine her own husband dying by suicide. The grieving process was long and painful. There were moments of despair after Jerry's death. Cindy would cry out to God, *Why me? Why Jerry?* However, Cindy realized that God was in control and had a plan that she did not understand at the time. She didn't understand why Jerry died and what that meant, but she was going to trust God.

Cindy volunteered as a chaplain for two law enforcement agencies. She used her own experiences to bring more awareness to the effects of the job on the mental health of police officers. She also united more families with husbands and dads who were police officers. She would meet with the wives for coffee and talk about their struggles and issues. Sharing stories together was effective and helpful, both for Cindy and for the other women, to know they were not alone.

Today, Cindy still misses Jerry, but she knows that he is now with God and that his suffering is over. She also knows that ultimately, God has a perfect plan, and she is willing to allow him to use her for his perfect plan, no matter what that entails.

Wise Counsel and Biblical Insight

Trials Will Come, Even More So to Believers

Pastor Paul Johnson says God watches over us no matter what is happening in our lives. "God is watching over these kinds of situations, and the Bible is very clear on that," Johnson said. "There are trials in life, but Jesus is there with us. God is always with us. God has a plan, and there's a tremendous future waiting for us as believers."

God Has a Perfect Plan for Our Lives

Cindy never thought her husband would commit suicide until it actually happened. This turned her life upside down and made her question God at times. Why did God allow this to happen to her? To her husband? Afterward, Cindy realized that God's plan is still perfect, and beautiful things can happen out of tragedy and trauma.

God Blesses Those Who Persevere

"Blessed is the one who perseveres under trial because, having stood the test, that person will receive the crown of life that the Lord has promised to those who love him" (James 1:12 NIV).

PRAYER

Dear Lord, I am experiencing a very difficult trial. I know that you told us these storms would happen in our lives, but I don't know how I can keep going. Give me the strength to persevere through this time in my life. I trust that you have a perfect plan for me. Amen.

Day 3

FROM LOSS TO HOPE

On Sunday mornings, it was easy to for Kayla to smile while she watched her husband, Andrew, preach. She would always sit in the front pew at church. She loved being a pastor's wife. Kayla met Andrew in college, and she knew in her heart he was the man of her dreams. They got married young, and they both jumped into ministry. Andrew's father started a church, and both Kayla and Andrew helped out there with different behind-the-scenes tasks.

For Kayla, she was living her dream life. She had everything she could ever want. She was blessed with three boys. Life was full, and life was busy. Kayla even entertained the idea of writing a devotional, and she shared the idea with her husband. She started a blog, and when Andrew's father was diagnosed with leukemia and became sick, she began to post some of her thoughts about his struggles. However, her busy life prevented her from really pursuing the idea further, so she put it on hold.

When Andrew's father passed away, Andrew was given the leadership position at their church. Although they grieved the loss of his father, Andrew and Kayla were both very hopeful about their future. However, Andrew started having panic attacks, and they became more and more frequent. They became debilitating, and over time, it was apparent that he would not be able to continue preaching in his condition. One massive panic attack landed him in the hospital. That's when the doctors informed Kayla that they had diagnosed her husband with depression. She was shocked. She never saw that coming, but with the assurance from the doctors, Kayla was confident he would be just fine with therapy and rest.

Andrew spent the next couple of months on sabbatical at home. He took medication and saw a therapist every week while Kayla did her best to take care of their boys without her husband's help. During Andrew's sickness, Kayla felt like God was so distant. She would pray, *Where are you God? Why aren't you fixing this man who has served you with his life? Why are you allowing anxiety?* Kayla would ask, *Why are you allowing depression?* But God seemed silent.

Finally, Andrew's health seemed like it was improving, and he went back to work. For a moment, everything seemed to be getting better. But again, his mental health went into a tailspin, and everyone around him realized he was not ready to come back to work and needed more time off.

While Kayla her kids were away from him for a short time, Andrew attempted suicide. He was rushed to the hospital, but there was nothing the doctors could do for him. Andrew was taken off life support, and Kayla and her boys spent time with him in his final moments.

After he died, Kayla was stunned and wrestled with God even more. *Really? Really, God?* she cried out. *First his father and now him? How could you allow this to happen?*

Her life was now completely different. She was a widow and a single mother of three boys. Kayla was grounded in her faith and knew that Andrew was in heaven. However, despite being raised in the church and spending her life in ministry,

Kayla experienced the presence of God in a completely new and profound way after the death of her husband. She began to notice that the little things in life were not so little anymore. God began doing small miracles in her life and the lives of her children.

One day while driving, Kayla was struck by the beauty of the sunset and pulled over to the side of the road. As she stared at the sunset, the Holy Spirit filled her up, and she felt as if she was sitting there with God. Another time she had been sitting at the kitchen table coloring with her son. A friend had given them a coloring book that described how the process of grief is like the process of the caterpillar changing from an egg to a caterpillar to chrysalis to butterfly. This simple coloring book was a beautiful example for both Kayla and her son. After coloring, it was nap time, so Kayla went over to the window to close the curtains, and there was a tiny caterpillar at the top of the curtain. Kayla had never seen a caterpillar in her house before. She showed it to her son, and he said, "It's a miracle from God."

God provided for her and her kids as people began to donate to a GoFundMe page that supported them financially and helped them get through some hardships. Friends would come over and pray with her and cry with her. Despite all the grief and pain, Kayla could clearly see the work of God in her life. This inspired her to go back to working on the devotional she had put off before. She already had a blog set up, so she began writing…and the words just flowed. Every emotion, question, and thought she had at that time came out.

Her writing caught the attention of several publishers and agents, and she received offers for book deals. She wrote her book about her journey through grief from a place of pain and loss. She shared what she learned about having hope in life after you've lost everything you ever wanted. Most importantly, she wrote about how God was always there through it all, even when he seemed distant.

Wise Counsel and Biblical Insight

God Is Working Even When We Don't See It

Pastor Paul Johnson says that we can experience peace beyond understanding even in times of pain and suffering. "People who are suffering right now can take heart and say, 'You know, God is working. It might not feel like it at the moment, but God is still with me.'"

God Will Always Reveal Himself in Times of Grief

During her husband's sickness, Kayla wrestled with God, asking where he was and why he wouldn't fix her husband. After her husband's death, Kayla experienced God in a completely new way, which showed her that he had never abandoned her.

God Is the God of Comfort

"Do not fear, for I am with you; do not be dismayed, for I am your God. I will strengthen you and help you; I will uphold you with my righteous right hand" (Isaiah 41:10 NIV).

PRAYER

Dear Lord, I don't know where you are during my time of grief and pain. You feel so distant and quiet. I believe your Word, and I believe you are still working in my life. Please give me the strength to get through this time. Amen.

Day 4

LOSING A WIFE

As I drove home to meet with my children, I wondered what I would tell them this time. It seemed far too familiar. Just a year ago I told them that their mother had breast cancer. Now, after a year's worth of treatment that we all thought was successful, I would inform them she had a year to live.

As a husband, father, and pastor, it had been a hellish year. Not only was I shepherding my wife and young children through the many emotions and fears that come with cancer, but I also dealt with a large church family that cared deeply for us but didn't always express it in ways that were helpful.

It felt like our church of two thousand gave me about that many ways to cure cancer and twice as many opinions about how to deal with it. People would leave brochures on my office chair, constantly nag me about going to Mexico for treatment or tell me about an ever-popular German clinic that could do miracles. But my wife, Jodee, wanted none of that. She was at peace. We had good doctors, and she simply wanted to spend this time with her family.

As I look back on that time in my life, and as I have walked through other losses, I have developed an acute aware-ness of the damage that well-meaning people can do in times of crisis. So often when we encounter pain, we immediately want to fix it. We want our friend or loved one to snap back to normal. We grieve the loss of the person we once knew. But that's not God's plan. He doesn't want the hurting person to resume their normal life. He wants to change them, grow them, deepen them, and show himself to them in ways they never dreamed. So we need to be okay with the new person who emerges from tragedy.

There's no doubt that I was changed by these two years. A friend once told me, "You'll be sadder but wiser." That was true. Jesus emerged from the pain. He gave me the strength to be a caregiver when, frankly, I had no idea what I was doing. He gave me the right words to say to my children. He provided the right people to come alongside us who didn't make demands and were simply present. That's the key to walking with a loved one through tragedy: just be present. Presence is what they need far more than Bible verses or a reminder that the one who has died is in heaven.

I also learned that Jesus is always present in our darkest hours. After scurrying around to plan funerals and wrap up Jodee's hospice care, the reality of her death hit hard. I would lie in bed at night trying not to think. But my mind raced. The loneliness was almost unbearable. But when I felt most alone, God visited me. I wasn't really alone at all. I can't explain exactly what God's presence feels like at these moments, but it's tangible. It's unmistakable, and I've learned to trust that it doesn't come and go. It's always there.

Trauma can be brutal. It scars. It has physical effects. It isolates. It strips away the best parts of our personality. It creates anxiety and fear. Our sense of security disappears. We feel trapped. Hope is hard to find. But my hope, and your hope, is that God is intimately involved with all of it.

The Father sent his only Son to experience the worst kind of trauma in order to save us. Jesus withstood terrible humiliation and unimaginable pain. He took upon himself the sins of everyone who ever inhabits this planet. He willingly did this so that all who believe in him can have eternal life. I can't comprehend the weight of that. But because he experienced it, he is a High Priest who loves you, understands you, cheers for you, protects you, prays for you, weeps with you, and laughs with you. You are not alone.

I finally arrived home, and I still didn't know how I would tell my kids that their mom was going to die. God prompted me to be honest. So, I spit it out. We all cried. We made it. We'll never be the same again. Death left us wounded, but it also gave us the opportunity to grow.

The pain of that experience is something that I wouldn't wish on anyone else. But I am thankful that I learned new things about Jesus. I love him more than ever. I trust him at a deeper level. I've given my life fully to him. Maybe it's time for you to do the same. Your High Priest is the safest, warmest, most encouraging person in the universe. Turn to him. He's waiting for you.

Wise Counsel and Biblical Insight

You Have a High Priest Who Loves You

"For we do not have a high priest who is unable to empathize with our weaknesses, but we have one who has been tempted in every way, just as we are—yet he did not sin. Let us then approach God's throne of grace with confidence, so that we may receive mercy and find grace to help us in our time of need" (Hebrews 4:15–16 NIV).

You Are Never Alone

"For I am convinced that neither death nor life, neither angels nor demons, neither the present nor the future, nor any powers, neither height nor depth, nor anything else in all creation, will be able to separate us from the love of God that is in Christ Jesus our Lord" (Romans 8:38–39 NIV).

Turn to God and You Will Find Him Waiting for You

"Why do some persons 'find' God in a way that others do not? Why does God manifest His Presence to some and let multitudes of others struggle along in the half-light of imperfect Christian experience? Of course, the will of God is the same for all. He has no favorites within His household. All He has ever done for any of His children He will do for all His children. The difference lies not with God but with us."[1]

PRAYER

Dear Lord, life can be dark and scary. Sometimes, I don't know what to do. But you are always there. Help me to learn to turn directly to you. Protect me from falling back into my old habits. May you and you only be my source of wisdom, joy, and peace. Amen.

---

1   A. W. Tozer, *The Pursuit of God* (Harrisburg, PA: Christian Publications, 1948), 65.

Section 2

LOSS OF A MARRIAGE

Day 5

GOD'S STEADFAST LOVE

Suzie was sure she had met the man of her dreams. He was a handsome, young football player who participated in church activities. She saw herself building a life with this man. Best of all, he was a follower of Jesus. He seemed committed to Christ, and Suzie fell in love with him. She married him when she was nineteen years old.

Suzie and her husband started a family by having two daughters. They participated in many church activities. She taught Sunday school, and he was a superintendent at a Christian school. He seemed to do all the right things, and the marriage was going great…until Suzie discovered that her husband was having a series of affairs with other women.

Suzie and her husband went through some marriage counseling and talked to their pastor. She asked others to pray for her and her marriage, that it could be restored in some way. Divorce was something she never imagined herself going through. But her husband refused to go any further with the counseling, so they had one last talk with their pastor. It was clear that her husband did not want to continue the marriage. They had been married eighteen years. He moved out of their marital home and moved in with another woman.

The experience was extremely painful for Suzie and her two daughters. Not only did she lose her husband and her daughters lose their father, but they also lost their home. She could not keep afloat financially, and she went through bankruptcy. Life just seemed to unravel in all kinds of ways: her husband was gone, she was no longer a wife, she lost her home, and she felt abandoned by God. How could this happen to her? What had she done to deserve this?

Resentment toward her husband built up, and finding forgiveness for him in her heart seemed impossible at the time. She struggled to envision a future for herself and her family. But God brought a wonderful man into Suzie's life. He was wise and loving and had three children of his own. They married, and their children blended very well.

However, Suzie's divorce with her first husband continued to have a big impact on her daughters. Her youngest daughter, Sarah, was twelve when her father left, and she began acting out at the age of fourteen. She started smoking, sneaking out of the house, and getting involved in unhealthy relationships. At the age of fifteen, she started drinking and would get drunk with her friends.

When Sarah was sixteen, she and her older sister, Lisa, were involved in a very serious car crash. Sarah, who didn't have a license, was driving at the time, and she suffered a serious brain injury from the accident. The doctors found out that she was pregnant, and she delivered a baby six months after the accident. Sarah put the baby up for adoption, which was a huge loss for Suzie's family.

After high school, Sarah packed her bags and moved out to Colorado to live with a young man she had met on a vacation. That didn't last, and two months later, she moved to

Texas to live with another man. Sarah was later diagnosed with bipolar disorder, and after years of praying, Suzie was blessed to have her daughter eventually return to live with her. They found a sober house to place her in, and Sarah found the Lord there and began to share her faith with others.

Sarah had struggled with many things through her life, but she had finally found traction. She made dramatic changes to build a solid recovery and a renewed relationship with Christ. She was passionate about living for Jesus, and her family had great hope for Sarah's future. Sarah found ways to influence others through her new life and an amazing church community where she participated in the recovery ministry, helping others find a path to sobriety. She also discovered a new love of prayer and would take every opportunity she could to stop and pray with people.

The threat of addiction never fully goes away, and two years after Sarah found sobriety and renewed her relationship with Christ, Suzie received a call that Sarah had died of an overdose. It was a complete shock. This experience caused Suzie to learn about God's steadfast love for her and her daughter, whom the Lord had a relationship with despite her addiction. Suzie realized that God had always been there, through her divorce, through all the pain, through her daughter's struggles. He was always there and never abandoned her or her family.

Later on, Suzie learned from others about the kind of impact her daughter had on them because Sarah shared her story and her faith. After her daughter's death, Suzie questioned how God could be good, but after hearing about what her Sarah was able to accomplish in such a short period of time, it was now clear that Suzie could not doubt God and what he was capable of doing in someone's life, no matter how far they strayed.

God was good to Suzie and her family, and now Suzie serves as an ordained pastor and counselor and is well-equipped to help others through their times of suffering.

Wise Counsel and Biblical Insight

Suffering Comes from a Fallen World, Not the Nature of God

Jessica Teresi, an advocate for sexual abuse survivors, says suffering is expected in this lifetime, and our fallen world does not reflect the true nature of God. "I think a lot of people have amazing relationships with God in their suffering because there's a lot of solace or comfort that comes," Jessica said. "For me, healing and suffering, they aren't a destination as much as they are just part of the journey of life. We live in a fallen world. We live in a world where we're constantly being pulled and pushed, and that is the nature of the world, not the nature of God."

God's Love Is Steadfast

Suzie could not understand why she was going through the trials she faced, such as her divorce, bankruptcy, and the death of her daughter. There were times when she questioned God and even felt abandoned by him. But over the years, she learned about God's steadfast love and how he had never abandoned her but instead brought many blessings into her life, with a new, loving husband and the opportunity to help others who face the same struggles.

Our Hope Is in God, Not Our Plans

"Those who hope in the Lord will renew their strength. They will soar on wings like eagles; they will run and not grow weary, they will walk and not be faint" (Isaiah 40:31 NIV).

PRAYER

Dear Lord, I am grieving the loss of my marriage. I don't know what lies ahead, and I am scared and depressed. I feel like my life is over and there is no life ahead of me. Please fill me with your love, the only love that really matters, and give me the strength to go on. I know you have a plan for me. Amen.

Day 6

ABUSED

For Lynda, it seemed like the same cycle every time. She would go on some dates, find the guy she thought was "the one," and get married. Then things would change, and her husband would turn into somebody else. The result was always the same: abuse and divorce.

The topic of abuse was something Lynda was familiar with. She grew up in a home where her parents physically abused one another. She didn't let that keep her down though. She went to college, and she eventually became an executive for a large international company, making good money and traveling the world. However, as a successful woman in the business world, Lynda experienced abuse in the workplace and, eventually, in her future marriages.

She was very young the first time she married. Lynda grew up Catholic, and divorce was heavily frowned upon, so she was serious about finding a good husband. She dated her first husband for five years before getting married. However, his behavior started to change, and he became very controlling of Lynda, telling her she needed to quit her job and stay at home.

After divorcing him, Lynda married her second husband and was determined to make it work. She did not want to face another divorce and the stigma that came with that from the church. The marriage started out great. It was very loving, but then it quickly moved into something dark.

Her second husband was introduced to pornography and wanted Lynda to take part as a way to enhance their sexual experience. The marriage turned into perversion, and he fell into a full-blown sexual addiction, calling sex lines and acting out behind her back. He was admitted into a treatment program and started seeing a counselor. Lynda thought having a family would "fix" him.

However, even with a family and a wife that would do anything to save the marriage, her husband could not break free from his addiction. Lynda turned to a church counselor for help, but he pointed at things that she was possibly doing wrong. It took twenty years for Lynda to finally come to terms with the fact that she had to divorce him.

After her second divorce, she went on thirty dates in thirty days and looked for a Christian husband. She found a guy that checked all her boxes, and he seemed like a great Christian man. After marrying him, she discovered later that he was seeing his ex-wife and having massage parlor sex. He also began to abuse Lynda in various ways: verbally, emotionally, and physically.

In all, Lynda underwent thirty-three surgeries from the physical abuse she endured during her failed marriages. She also contracted sexual diseases from them, which left her with severe pain. The constant abuse she endured over the years led to depression and post-traumatic stress. After divorcing her husband, Lynda was a single mom. She was taking care of her kids alone when she decided to get her master's degree in counseling, even though she was still working as an executive.

God started doing a good work in Lynda. Instead of blaming her ex-husbands for what had happened to her, she started to look in the mirror to see what was really going on with her. She began seeing a Christian counselor twice a week for five years, and that helped her rewire her identity away from the stigma that came from being a three-time divorcee. She was baptized, and she accepted Christ at a different level than before. She was redeemed.

Afterward, Lynda began talking to a man who was one of her previous "thirty dates in thirty days." During that time, he had told her that she was "un-dateable" and that she needed help. But now, they renewed their friendship, and that turned into a romance. They married three and a half years later, and nothing but blessings have come to Lynda from this Christ-centered relationship.

Her loving husband encouraged her to use her counseling degree, and she decided to leave the corporate world to become a Christian therapist. She wanted to practice in the areas in which she was most experienced: sexual addiction and abuse. Lynda now has her own counseling practice and helps other women who experience abuse and women whose husbands have a sexual addiction.

Wise Counsel and Biblical Insight

God Can Redeem Anyone

Jessica Teresi, an advocate for sexual abuse survivors, says God can redeem anyone who has been abused. "I believe that God redeems us all, and I believe that we have to want that, but I believe a part of that is that we have to take accountability for our decisions," Jessica says.

Abuse Erases Identity; God Replaces It

The more she was abused over the years, the more Lynda lost her identity and her sense of worth and value. This created a cycle that fed itself with more abuse. It wasn't until she stepped back and allowed herself to spend important time in Christ to see that she was a special creation in his image and that God always had a plan for her life despite her past and failed marriages.

God Is a Champion for the Abused

"For he has not despised or scorned the suffering of the afflicted one; he has not hidden his face from him but has listened to his cry for help" (Psalm 22:24 NIV).

PRAYER

Dear Lord, I have been abused and battered. I am full of guilt and shame for what has happened to me, and I feel no sense of worth. I know you have a plan for my life, and I know my life has meaning because Jesus died for me. Please reveal your purpose for me. Amen.

Section 3

LOSS OF A
YOUNG CHILD

HATING GOD'S PLAN

God called Dan to ministry when he was a junior in high school. Over the years he served in a variety of ways from a worship leader to a youth pastor to a church planter. As he got deeper into ministry, he and his wife were expecting their first child, a girl. They were both so excited. They planned on naming their baby girl Louisa Hope. As his wife was close to giving birth, the couple asked about scheduling a day to induce labor, but the doctor recommended that they wait another week.

They came back to the hospital the following Monday, again very excited to see their child. However, something was wrong, very wrong. The doctors could not find a heartbeat. Dan learned the news that their child had died. He could not believe what he was hearing. After hearing what had happen, Dan demanded that the doctors get the baby out of his wife as quickly as possible, but the doctors recommended that his wife go through with the birthing process.

The labor was long and painful for his wife, and seeing that was horrible for Dan. To him, it felt like an out-of-body experience. He was watching his wife give birth to their baby girl, knowing she would not experience life on earth. Afterward, Dan held the baby for a long time. The nurse asked him if he wanted to have his picture taken with the baby.

At first, he thought that was very strange, but he ended up allowing her to take the picture.

The birth was an extremely difficult experience for both Dan and his wife. His wife developed a high level of anxiety. It became so intense, in fact, that she had to start taking anxiety medication. For Dan, being a worship leader at the time was hard. Even though he was not angry at God for his daughter's death, he could not find it in himself to *really* praise God, even though he still showed up at church and led worship.

He knew that he should trust God and his plan, but deep down inside he hated that plan. *Why did God allow this? Why did God cause this?* Dan would ask himself over and over again.

Even though he had a job in worship ministry, Dan had to relearn how to praise God. He had to relearn the wonderful things God had done in his life, despite the challenges and painful times. As he and his wife walked through the difficult weeks and months after their daughter's death, they decided to not be fake or put on a "mask" in front of others at church. They decided to be real about their feelings, emotions, and thoughts.

Dan was a candidate for a position as a new pastor at a church. He preached there, and afterward, they allowed time for the congregation to ask him and his wife questions. His wife opened up and told them about the death of their daughter and how the experience had left her with extreme anxiety that she now took medication to control. From that moment on, God really started to work in Dan's life. He learned some important lessons about grief, death, and God himself. He learned about grace and what it *really* meant to walk alongside someone experiencing a loss. This helped him even more in his role as a chaplain for his local police department.

God has blessed Dan and his wife with two children, and today, Dan is a pastor at a multi-campus church. Every now and then, Dan still looks at the pictures of him holding Louisa Hope on that painful day at the hospital. Now, he can look at them and realize how God was always there alongside him with a special plan for his life.

Wise Counsel and Biblical Insight

Grief Comes to Everyone, Including Leaders

Therapist Allie Dietert says it is completely normal to question God when hit with grief after losing a loved one. "Isaiah 53:3 prophesized that Jesus was a man 'acquainted with deepest grief,'" Dietert said, quoting the New Living Translation. "If you look all through the Psalms, you will see how often they refer to David as a man after God's own heart, and so many of the songs are just colored with David complaining, crying out to God, begging God, asking him, '*God why me, God why aren't you listening to me*?' And I think people need to hear that validation from a spiritual leader. That not only is grief okay, that grief is the universal experience of all people, including Jesus Christ, who was the ultimate human being. He was 'acquainted with grief,' it says in the Bible, with 'the deepest grief,' so just tell people to kind of befriend the experience and embrace it and allow this experience."

God Is in Control When We Are in Doubt

After his daughter's death, Dan struggled to praise God. He had no idea what God had in store for him after that painful experience, and it took a long time for him to see that God was always in control.

God Is the Father of Compassion, the God of All Comfort

"Praise be to the God and Father of our Lord Jesus Christ, the Father of compassion and the God of all comfort, who comforts us in all our troubles, so that we can comfort those in any trouble with the comfort we ourselves receive from God" (2 Corinthians 1:3–4 NIV).

PRAYER

Dear Lord, I am torn from the loss of a loved one. I don't know what to do with all this grief and pain. Please comfort me during this time. Although I have questions and doubts, I know you are in control. Amen.

Day 8

BLAMING GOD

Rick and his wife were expecting a child, and they were very excited. He worked in the restaurant industry, and she worked in the telecom industry. His wife entertained the idea of being a stay-at-home mother, but they both agreed that she would continue to work for a little while after maternity leave.

Rick couldn't wait to be a father and do all the things fathers do. His son, Calvin, was born, and it was a great moment for both Rick and his wife. The couple did diligent research on daycare providers, and they found one they liked. After twelve weeks of maternity leave, Rick's wife went back to work, and Calvin entered daycare. The plan was for Rick's wife to work six more months before transitioning over to being a stay-at-home mom.

One morning, Rick got a call from his wife, saying that another child had fallen on Calvin and that Calvin was being taken to the children's hospital by ambulance. Rick had no idea how serious the incident was until he got to the hospital. His wife and the daycare provider were already at the hospital when Rick arrived. A nurse took Rick into an examining room to see his son.

Rick stood next to the doctor when the doctor flashed a flashlight in Calvin's eyes. The doctor's facial expression suddenly darkened for a split second, and it was at that moment that Rick knew his son was dead. He went into shock and vomited in the restroom.

Family members gathered at the hospital to be with Rick and his wife. They spent the next forty hours waiting as doctors performed tests on their son. And then the police arrived. Homicide detectives told Rick that the doctors had concluded that Calvin's death was not accidental, but his death was the result of being shaken. It hadn't even dawned on Rick until that moment that the daycare provider had left the hospital.

When Rick, his wife, and some of their family walked away from the hospital, they felt numb. Even with all the support they received, the couple had no idea the lasting impact their infant's death would have on them. From then on, Rick would live in his life as if he was coming in and out of a fog. The couple reached for solutions in an attempt to escape their grief. Soon after Calvin's death, in an attempt to recovery some sense of life, Rick's wife asked to have more children. Nine and a half months later, they had a beautiful baby girl, another son a couple of years later, and finally another daughter. Those children were and are a blessing, but they did not fix the grief that remained after losing Calvin. Rick and his wife were both big readers and had a large collection of books in their home. But not one Bible. Neither of them was a Christian or spiritual in any way. The only concept Rick had of God was that he was an angry God and would throw lightning bolts at him if he messed up too badly. It was pretty easy for him to exclude God from his life.

Rick grew up without a father and learned how to be independent at an early age. He transformed his survival skills into business skills, and he eventually owned his own business and made a lot of money. However, making more money fed an addictive lifestyle, and after losing Calvin, Rick also began to drink more. His drinking got to the point to where he would pull up to a liquor store and the employees would help him wheel out six cases of beer every week. His drinking was out of control and that would have an impact on his marriage.

He isolated himself more and more from his wife and others in his life. She tried to communicate with him, but he blew those attempts off. His mother-in-law suggested that Rick go talk to a pastor. But that just made Rick more upset at pastors and churches in general—and at God. The death of his son gave him another excuse for blaming God. He was unable to love God and unable to love himself.

His job became boring to him, and he began trading in the foreign currencies market, a very risky way of gambling. It grew into a full-blown gambling addiction along with his drinking. Finally, his wife left him, and Rick found himself at the lowest point of his life. He felt he had run out of options, so Rick went to Alcoholics Anonymous, and through its twelve-step program, Rick finally realized he had been carrying a load of guilt over his son's death. Rick now knew that he had been grieving his son's death through drinking, gambling, and isolating.

Over time, Rick found God right there with him even after years of rejection. Rick knew that his grieving was unique to him, and only God could help and heal him. It took a long time, but looking back, Rick realized how much God always loved him and his son. At the time of Calvin's death, Rick and his wife agreed to have him be an organ donor. That decision saved seven other children's lives.

Wise Counsel and Biblical Insight

God Is There, Even for the Grieving Unbelievers

Pastor Paul Johnson says God is there for even those who do not accept him during their time of grieving or loss. "That's a great message for people who may think that just because they are not understanding God or they are not feeling God or God seems to be distant, that God is not there. But God is still very much involved, all the time," Johnson said. "You might not even know it at the point of crisis. Now you look back and go, 'Wow, God was in this whole thing.'"

God's Timing Is Always Different Than Ours

Rick never would have expected his baby boy to die by murder at a daycare. This traumatic event turned his life upside down, but even though it took a long time, even though he was angry at God for years and years, Rick eventually found a deep love for God. Now, Rick shares his story with others in hopes that they can find hope in their times of grieving.

God Is Our Rock and Redeemer

"May these words of my mouth and this meditation of my heart be pleasing in your sight, Lord, my Rock and my Redeemer" (Psalm 19:14 NIV).

PRAYER

Dear Lord, I am grieving, and to be honest, I am angry at you for letting this happen. I know you are listening to me, and I know you love me regardless. Please fill me with your love as I know only you can heal me from this pain I am experiencing. Amen.

Day 9

LOSS AND FORGIVENESS

Stephanie could not wait for the last day of school. As a teacher, this meant that she would be able to spend the entire summer with her baby boy, Dylan. While she was teaching, Dylan spent time at Laurie's, his babysitter who was a great friend of Stephanie. Laurie was better than a friend, more like family. Stephanie had been dropping Dylan off at Laurie's since he was four months old. Laurie had grandchildren and loved Dylan like her own.

When the last day of school arrived, Stephanie was at school finishing up. She was turning in her grades when the principal came in and told her that she had a phone call from a hospital. At first, she was confused, and then her heart rate began accelerating. A man was on the other end, and Stephanie expected that he was a doctor. However, she quickly realized she was not speaking with a doctor. She had to interrupt the man to ask who he was again. He was a chaplain. At that moment, Stephanie's worst fear came true, and she fell to her knees crying.

She rushed to the hospital where Dylan was. When she told the receptionist who she was, the receptionist began crying and ushered Stephanie into one of the emergency bays where her son lay on a gurney. The nurses and doctors who were there with Dylan also appeared to have been crying. The chaplain came in and sat with Stephanie and confirmed that Dylan, who was ten months and ten days old, was gone. Stephanie's husband, Scott, arrived in a panic at the hospital, and both of them sat together in shock, absorbing the impossible news.

They met a heartbroken Laurie the next day to find out what happened to Dylan. She explained that Dylan had been playing in the sandbox with Laurie's two grandkids. Stephanie had asked Laurie to keep Dylan out of the sandbox because he would put the sand in his mouth and try to eat it. Laurie's grandkids had discovered Dylan not breathing, and that's when Laurie called 911.

The fact that Laurie still allowed Dylan to get in the sandbox after Stephanie had asked her not to was hard to hear for Stephanie, and as Laurie talked, bitterness and anger started to creep into Stephanie's heart. But she knew those feelings were toxic, and she knew she should not only forgive Laurie but also embrace her. Instead of lashing out, Stephanie then switched the conversation to what Dylan's last day was like. Laurie brightened and told her all the details of his day, the things he did that made her laugh, the little discoveries that delighted the child. Stephanie didn't know it at the time, but this was God's way of giving grace to Stephanie and allowing her to know what Dylan's life was like until the very end.

Not only did Stephanie miss Dylan, but she also missed being a mom. Losing her healthy baby seemed so unnatural, so brutal. For Stephanie, being a mother was her core identity. She had so much love to give her child that she couldn't give anymore. Every day after Dylan's death was excruciating. Everywhere Stephanie and her husband turned, there was something that reminded them of Dylan.

In a bold act of forgiveness, Stephanie and Scott invited Laurie to speak at Dylan's funeral. They did not have a home church at the time, and Laurie's church was welcoming to them and more than happy to accommodate them. Stephanie did not want bitterness to take hold of her, and having Laurie speak at the funeral was a part of the process of letting go of any bitterness toward Laurie for what happened. She had learned from the trauma she had been through before. Her parents divorced when she was young, then when she was ten years old, her father, a psychiatrist, was murdered by one of his patients. Stephanie knew that living in love and forgiveness was a better way to live, no matter how hard it was.

Stephanie and her husband tried for another child soon after Dylan's death, but she had a miscarriage seven months later. To her, that was like losing Dylan all over again. But God had amazing things in store for them.

They found a supportive church community to join, and Stephanie was given a whole new understanding of her son's death: Dylan's death was not something that happened *to her*, and God had made her a steward of Dylan's life, and that was a huge blessing. This helped her tremendously in healing from the pain. She was shown that it was her job to carry on Dylan's memory, and she did just that. Now, twenty-one years after his passing, people are still affected by his life and the memories of his life. Stephanie is now also able to minister to others who are on the same painful journey of losing a child.

As for her relationship with Laurie, Stephanie would go on to have two more children after Dylan and asked Laurie to babysit them. That was a beautiful and emotional moment for both of them. Trusting Laurie with her children was proof that God had healed Stephanie's heart.

Wise Counsel and Biblical Insight

God Has a Purpose for Everything

Pastor Paul Johnson says trials in our lives are meant to change us for the better. "When people are going through any kind of trauma, I think the lie that Satan puts in people's minds is that there is a normal that has been deviated from, and at some point, that person is going back to normal," Paul said. "But here's the lie in that. The Bible is very clear that trials are for a reason and for a purpose. What God is doing is refining, changing. God is preparing. God does not want us to go back to the way we were because he has a new mission for us based on who we are now."

God Gives Grace in Unexpected, Unique Ways

Even before Stephanie was plugged into God, he was orchestrating ways to show her grace after her son's death.

God Grants Peace to Us Even during the Chaos

"Praise be to the God and Father of our Lord Jesus Christ, the Father of compassion and the God of all comfort, who comforts us in all our troubles, so that we can comfort those in any trouble with the comfort we ourselves receive from God" (2 Corinthians 1:3–4 NIV).

PRAYER

Dear Lord, thank you for your wonderful grace and for giving me the capacity to go through this very difficult loss. Please continue to show me your love and purpose in all of this. Amen.

Section 4

LOSS OF AN ADULT CHILD

Day 10

THE LOSS THAT
NEVER STOPS

There's no way to describe the loss of a child in a way that does it justice. It's heart-wrenching, life-altering, and isolating. After the shock wears off, you began to realize that nothing will ever be the same. As I grieved the loss of this dear loved one, I also mourned a life that would never be the same again.

Taylor was a kind and gentle young man. My wife, Wendi, and I treasured him. His smile lit up a room and his wry sense of humor elicited joy. Everyone who came in contact with him immediately became his friend. He was adored by his brothers and sisters. He was a great kid. But now he's gone. He was murdered.

The word *murder* stops me in my tracks. What? That doesn't really happen, does it? I wondered: *Why would God allow someone to shoot Taylor dead while he was all alone? How could I possibly shepherd my family through this when I couldn't even keep myself together?* These are the questions that haunted me. These are the questions that still draw me to the heart of God because there is no other place to go.

Taylor was about to graduate from a school for the performing arts. He dreamed of being a record producer

54

and had met others with the same interests and goals. He formed a group that sought financing for a project, and unfortunately, money came from some unsavory sources. Unknowingly, Taylor was introduced to the dark underworld of the illegal drug trade. The people around him used him. His sweet innocence was an easy mark.

When one of his "friends" asked him to house-sit for a few days, he was overjoyed. As a starving student, a few dollars seemed like manna from heaven. The last text I got from him expressed thankfulness that this opportunity had presented itself. I would never see him again.

A group of men came to rob this house in the middle of the night. Taylor simply looked out the window to see what was happening. They shot him. While he lay gasping for breath, they walked right by him. The detectives assured us that he was in the wrong place at the wrong time.

Wendi was home when there came the knock on the door that every parent dreads. When the police told her the news, she and our entire family became victims of trauma. Our children had their brains literally rewired. Loss, violence, and the suddenness of Taylor's death tore the rug of security out from under us. We didn't know if we would ever feel safe again.

I wasn't sure I could continue to lead a church. Preaching seemed out of the question. I had no strength left to pastor anyone. A loving and caring congregation still needed me, but I knew that I wouldn't be the same pastor that I once was.

Wendi didn't know how she would be able shepherd our children through this. She'd lost a son, but small children still begged for her attention. How would she grieve? Who would she turn to? As a married couple, how would our love survive this?

These are real questions that those who are in trauma ask themselves. And for me, that answer is simple: *God is real.* Through all the questions, confusion, and extreme pain that still rampages through our home, God is present.

The Bible is very clear that the Lord does his best work during times of suffering. Though I couldn't move toward him, he pursued me. During sleepless nights he comforted me. He emerged in my dreams. He reminded me of his everlasting love through his Word and through the loving actions of others. Many of Taylor's friends were introduced to Jesus for the first time because they'd never faced anything like this before. Trauma is awful, but God is wonderful.

The thing about losing a child is that it never goes away. Wendi and I are different people now. Our kids have lost a brother whom they will never see again. But each of us, in our own way, has been confronted with the love of God. Why did he take Taylor from us? I don't know. I may never know in this lifetime. But I have grown to trust that this was somehow God's best plan. During the many times when I feel isolated and misunderstood, alone in my thoughts, privately grieving, sometimes even frustrated to the point of hopelessness, I have learned that I have nowhere to turn but toward God. And that's the way he wants it.

God knows that he's the best thing for me. He knows that in order for me to find healing, joy, hope, and peace, it must come from him. Trauma forces me to confront God every day. And as I wrestle with him, I love him more deeply. I trust him more than ever. My faith has been deeply rooted. I am preaching from a heart of empathy and real-life experience. Wendi mentors dozens of women who turn to her because she understands their struggles.

When tragedy strikes or the ordinary burdens of the day begin to press in on you, remember that God is present. He loves you. He is working to make you more like him. Struggle and pain are gifts. The Lord uses them to refine his children whom he loves so deeply. Turn to Jesus. He is waiting for you.

Wise Counsel and Biblical Insight

Suffering Is Meant to Strengthen You

"Consider it pure joy, my brothers and sisters, whenever you face trials of many kinds, because you know that the testing of your faith produces perseverance. Let perseverance finish its work so that you may be mature and complete, not lacking anything" (James 1:2–4 NIV).

Trials Help You to Be More Like Christ

"The God of all grace, who called you to his eternal glory in Christ, after you have suffered a little while, will himself restore you and make you strong, firm and steadfast" (1 Peter 5:10 NIV).

Trauma Ultimately Brings New Life

"Dark clouds bring waters, when the bright bring none."[2]

---

2   John Bunyan, *The Pilgrim's Progress* (Buffalo: George H. Derby and Co., 1853), see Christian Classics Ethereal Library, https://www.ccel.org/b/bunyan/progress/pilgrim1.html.

PRAYER

Dear Lord, I often doubt your love. I want to run away from my pain. But you are always there, always loving, forever patient, unfathomably kind. Teach me to trust you, knowing that you have my best interest in mind. You are my God. I will love you forever. Amen.

Day 11

A DAUGHTER'S PAIN, A MOTHER'S PAIN

The train horn was getting louder and louder. Kim and her brother and sister just sat in the car quietly as their mother gripped the steering wheel. Their car was sitting on the railroad tracks on a rural road in Missouri. What was happening? As the train got closer, Kim's mother let out a deep sigh, put the car back in drive, and rolled off the tracks.

This moment never left Kim, and it showed how her mother suffered from deep depression, enough to even consider ending her life along with her children's lives. The pain from her husband divorcing her was almost too much to bear, and that is why she drove her car onto the tracks with her kids inside. She felt like she couldn't live any longer, and she didn't want her children to suffer without her. Mental illness is real and dangerous if left untreated, something Kim knew too well from an early age. Despite what happened that day on the railroad tracks, Kim knew her mother loved her and her siblings.

Her mom was a hand model. So, when Kim was born, her mother was devastated to discover that her newborn baby girl was missing three fingers. Every mother wants her baby to be healthy and perfect. A baby missing three fingers was a big problem for Kim's mom, and she struggled with coming to terms with it. Nevertheless, even with her bouts of depression, Kim's mom was a godly and loving woman.

When Kim was six years old, her father explained to her mother why their daughter had been born with missing fingers. He had just learned that scientists had discovered that an anti-nausea drug called Thalidomide, common in the 1950s for pregnant women, was causing babies to be born with missing limbs, arms, legs, and fingers. Even though her mom was not to blame for Kim's missing fingers, this was horrible news for her mother, and she began to struggle mentally even more.

Soon after the incident with the train, Kim's mother entered a mental hospital in Cincinnati, Ohio, where she would stay the rest of her life. Kim and her siblings went to live with their faither and stepmother. When Kim was seventeen years old, her mother committed suicide. It was very difficult for Kim to lose her mother, but she tried to be strong and was determined to make something of her life. She met her husband, Jim, in college, and she became a dentist and practiced alongside her husband. They started a family, and things seemed to be going great.

Life for Kim hit a bump when her husband was diagnosed with liver cancer in 2007. Fortunately, he was able to receive a liver transplant. However, Kim's world came crashing down when her only son, Eric, took his own life. This was a complete shock to Kim and her family. She didn't know how to process the loss, and it sent her down a dark road of guilt, shame, and depression.

Eric was attending Columbia University and was a brilliant jazz musician. He was dating someone, and they had a breakup. He took his own life forty-five minutes after that. Kim was shattered. Her son's suicide triggered dark and troubling emotions she had stored deep inside her since her mother took her own life decades before. Thoughts and accusations roared through her head: *Maybe I could have saved him. Maybe I could have saved my mother. Maybe they are gone because of something I did…or didn't do.* She reasoned that the common denominator between her son and her mother was *herself.* That conclusion and the guilt it carried had a devastating effect on Kim.

The grief was heavy, and as hard as she tried to keep it from pushing her down, some days all she could manage was to find a place to cry and let her emotions go. She lost her mother, her son, and now she felt like she was losing her identity… mostly as a mother.

With the help of her church, friends, and family, Kim was able to navigate through grief and learn that even God grieves for his children. He even grieved the death of his own son.

Years later, Kim was having a conversation with a friend who was on the board of Books for Africa, an organization that starts libraries in poverty-stricken areas. Kim decided she wanted to start a library in Rwanda in Eric's name. For Kim, the experience was amazing. She was able to meet people in a country that was flooded with grief after a bloody genocide. She could relate to those around her, and it was a healing moment that she never could have imagined.

Now, years after her son's death, Kim has a closer relationship with God and a deeper understanding that grief is something God gives us to cope with sudden and painful losses in our lives.

Wise Counsel and Biblical Insight

Trauma Alters Us

Counselor Tom Colbert says trauma, like the trauma Kim experienced in losing both her mother and her son to suicide, can alter the way we think about life in general. Depression and guilt can settle in, and we may start telling ourselves lies. Colbert describes all trauma as denaturing; in other words, trauma changes or destroys the characteristics that make us who we are. This type of negative transformation happens as a result of severe trauma but also from the smaller traumas in life that we sometimes gloss over, such as the loss of a job, the heartbreak of a breakup, a bad medical report, and so on.

Peace Is Always Found in Christ

"Therefore, since we have been justified through faith, we have peace with God through our Lord Jesus Christ" (Romans 5:1 NIV).

PRAYER

Dear Lord, my grief, shame, and guilt are weighing me down and crushing me. Please give me the peace I need that can only be found in your love. Amen.

Day 12

GRIEF AS A COMPANION

Brad jumped from a tranquil sleep, awakened by what sounded like someone knocking on his door. It was late at night, and he wondered who it could be. He hurried cautiously to the door. As he looked through the door to see who it was, he was surprised to see two police officers. His body went cold as his mind raced to figure out why they might be there. He quickly accounted for which of his four kids were home and which ones were not. He opened the door. The somber officers asked to step inside the home. What happened next changed Brad's life forever. "We found your son, Logan, dead in a motel room," the officers told him. At the age of twenty-five, Logan had taken his own life.

For Brad, everything just stopped. The whole world around him came to a halt. Questions swirled through his mind. And then, slowly, he had to process everything in his life. He couldn't even decipher his emotions, whether he was sad or angry. Then he had to think about the other people in his life and Logan's life. Logan had a fiancée, and this would be devastating for her. He had to think how he was going to tell his other sons about Logan's death. He also had to tell Logan's own son, who lived with Brad while Logan was attending Teen

Challenge, a faith-based rehabilitation program, to fight a drug addiction. Logan's son was about to turn six years old.

Brad also started to question himself as a parent. Why would his son end his own life? Was there anything he could have done differently to keep it from happening? Brad and his wife were Christians who raised four kids. Logan, their oldest, eventually became a Christian as well. But his life was messy. He and his girlfriend started using drugs, and he struggled with drugs before becoming a Christian and after. Logan knew he had to do something to address this problem, and that was when he went to Teen Challenge, leaving his young son with his parents.

But Logan's suicide hit Brad like a ton of bricks. He was not expecting it at all and had no idea what to do with his pain. Brad received support from several people in his life, like his father, who told him that Logan's death was not his fault. Brad's boss also called him in to tell him how sorry he was for Brad's loss and that his own son had also died. He told Brad that as a fellow Christian, he believed that they would both see their sons again someday. Even with all that support, there was one thing that seemed to never leave Brad alone…grief.

A few weeks after Logan's funeral, Brad's grandson asked if they could sleep in the living room together. Brad agreed under one condition, that his grandson would go to sleep within fifteen minutes. If not, Brad said, he would have to go back to his bedroom. His grandson was out cold in no time.

Brad ended up spending a restless night on the couch. He finally fell asleep, and in a vivid dream, he saw a figure. It was a figure of a man coming up to the window, and then the man was standing at the foot of the couch. He was about nine feet tall, and his head was down, his shoulders slouched. The figure held out his hand to Brad, who was reluctant to take it. He knew who this was. It was Grief. Brad did not want to go with him. He knew the company Grief kept. He didn't want to go down the road of depression, isolation, and all the other terrible places Grief would take him. But Grief just stood there, waiting.

After what seemed like eternity, Brad finally gave in. Right when he touched the figure's hand, he found himself on an unfamiliar street, and there were several other streets going in different directions with names like "Anger," "Depression," and "Helplessness." Brad looked down the street of Anger and saw that it was filled with houses with their lights on, but there were no curtains on the windows. He could see in each house, and he could see all the strife and turmoil inside. Grief did not take him down that street. Instead, Brad followed him into a dark alley, holding him by the hand.

All of a sudden, Brad got knocked down to the ground by something behind him. It felt like he had been hit by a sledge-hammer in the back of the head. It was a barrage of questions and criticisms. *Why didn't you go visit him while he was staying alone in a motel room? You knew he was alone! Why didn't you?*

Every time Brad got up, he got knocked down again. He looked up at Grief, who was just standing there waiting on him. He looked past Grief and saw, at the end of the long alley, a light. He looked harder, and in the light was a park where the sun was shining. There were kids laughing and playing. Brad then realized that Grief was leading him there. Right then and there, he finally understood something incredible. Grief was not his enemy but rather his companion in a sense.

Because of Logan's death, Brad was never going to be the same. But even before he knew it, God was using this tragedy

65

for something good. Brad now had the experience, knowledge, and fortitude to encourage others who had lost a child.

This painful experience would ultimately bring Brad closer to God, and his relationship with the Lord strengthened. Even though he had a relationship with God before Logan's death, he now wanted to know God even more. Most importantly, through all the grief, he learned that real peace only comes from God and his Word.

Wise Counsel and Biblical Insight

Counselor Julie Hull on How We Perceive Grief

Acceptance of grief is often confused with the idea that we must be okay with what has happened. This is not the case at all. Those of us who have grieved will never be okay about this part of our story, and we would have never written it this way. This is about accepting that this new reality is a permanent reality. Brad realizes he will be forever changed by the reality of Logan's death, and his family will never be the same.

We cannot fix or take away another person's pain, but we are called as believers to lift each other up through the pain. It's often the broken that can speak to another's brokenness when no one else can get through. Brad has been compelled to use his pain and his story to come alongside those like him who have lived through a day when the whole world came to a halt.

God Gives Us His Peace

"Peace I leave with you; my peace I give you. I do not give to you as the world gives. Do not let your hearts be troubled and do not be afraid" (John 14:27).

PRAYER

Dear Lord, you have promised me peace and I need it. Help me to find it even when it looks like I am all alone. My heart is troubled, and I am afraid. Help me to trust you with my incredible pain. Help me in the next hour, day, week, and well into the future to stand on this promise. Amen.

A PART OF MYSELF IS GONE

Anarae was Mariana's only daughter and, now that she was an adult, was also Mariana's best friend. Anarae was intelligent, a tutor for elementary school kids, a lover of many genres of music, and an avid chess player. She had a heart for the under-dog and a strong desire to boost the spirits of kids and friends who were struggling in some manner. Mariana was Anarae's biggest fan. They completed each other's sentences and laughed at things no one else would understand. They discussed every-thing, argued, and solved the world's problems together.

One day, Mariana called Anarae several times but could not get a hold of her daughter. Hours turned to days, and days turned to a week. Anarae had gone missing, and the longer she was missing, the more Mariana feared the worst. Then Mariana got the call she was dreading. Anarae's remains had been discovered, and investigators determined that she had been murdered.

The gruesome details of her daughter's death kept Mariana from sleeping for many nights. *Why did they have to kill her? Why couldn't she have just been harmed?* Mariana would constantly ask herself. But the biggest question Mariana asked herself was, *How do I live without her?* Mariana felt like a large piece of her was ripped away. During her grief, she experienced many emotions, but most frequently, she was angry. She grew angrier the longer the trial for her daughter's murderers got put off, angrier at the perpetrators, and angrier at the legal system. Then she got into the blame game.

For a time, Mariana believed lies in her head about her daughter's death. Lies that if she had been a better parent or done things differently, Anarae would still be alive. She found herself in a sea of blame, anger, and disillusionment. She also wondered, *Where did God fit into any of this?* Nothing inspired her to pray. At the time, she didn't think prayer would do anything. She had already lost her daughter. Would prayer bring her back?

However, God put many people in Mariana's life who prayed for her and helped her move forward. Support poured in from people and places she had never heard of. One woman, who had lost a young son to cancer, gave her a packet of encouraging Bible verses. One day, Mariana looked in the packet and found a verse that she clung to: "The eyes of the Lord are on the righteous and his ears are attentive to their cry" (Psalm 34:15 NIV). The verse, for as short as it was, spoke volumes to Mariana. She now understood that the Lord was attentive to *her* cry, any time, day or night. Prayer had a whole new meaning.

Although the loss of Anarae was excruciating and painful for Mariana, she was able to reconnect with God, and her faith in him deepened.

Wise Counsel and Biblical Insight

God Helps Us Meet Unbearable Pain

People say that God doesn't give you more than you can handle. Often this conclusion is a misinterpretation of a passage from Paul in 1 Corinthians:

> No temptation has overtaken you except what is common to mankind. And God is faithful; he will not let you be tempted beyond what you can bear. But when you are tempted, he will also provide a way out so that you can endure it. (1 Corinthians 10:13 NIV)

God sometimes does give us more than we can handle, and he wants us to turn to him as our way through whatever it is that overwhelms us. There is suffering in life that we can't face on our own strength. He is always with us in the power of the Holy Spirit. That's the power that can sustain us through prayer.

Grieving Does Not Mean Something Is Wrong with You

Just as Satan tried to attack Jesus when he was vulnerable in the desert, he tries to attack us when we at our most vulnerable. He attacks us with doubts and lies about ourselves, others, life, and about God!

Mariana experienced one if the most vulnerable, despairing, agonizing, gnashing-of-teeth times a human being could ever experience, not just in the death of her daughter and best friend but also the tormenting hours of not knowing what had happened to her daughter.

Mariana's rage and blame had to go somewhere, and she experienced the roller coaster of extreme grief responses. Her feelings progressed through shock, denial, disbelief, outward rage at the murderer to guilt and shame, finally spiraling into sadness, depression, and loneliness.

As Mariana discovered, facing grief alone is overwhelming. But she discovered that God is always with us in our suffering. Sometimes it takes the actions of other people in our lives to see God's presence. We find healing when we surrender to his arms and allow ourselves to experience our grief with him.

God Grants Peace to Us Even during the Chaos

"The peace of God, which transcends all understanding, will guard your hearts and your minds in Christ Jesus" (Philippians 4:7 NIV).

PRAYER

Thank you, Jesus, for being acquainted with grief yourself and standing firm with me in mine. I may always feel the loss and grief for my loved one, but I am confident that with you, I will find a path through my grief. Amen.

Section 5

LOSS OF EXPECTATIONS

Day 14

THE DESTINATION OVERCOMES THE JOURNEY

Lemuel could not wait for his first day at a private school. His parents, who were both pastors, homeschooled him, and while that went well, he wanted to be around other kids in a Christian environment. Once his family moved to a big city, that opportunity opened up for him at the age of ten. At first, the fifth grade at the new school went great. He met some really nice kids that became his friends. However, there was one student in his new school who would change Lemuel's life in the worst way possible.

One of the older students, who claimed to be a Christian, began molesting other students in the school, and Lemuel would become one of his victims. It didn't just happen to him in the fifth grade, but it would happen again in the sixth grade, and then again in the seventh grade.

He tried to keep the abuse a secret because of the embarrassment attached to it, and he did for a long time. He was fearful of what others might think if he told them about it. He began to have flashbacks of the abuse he had experienced, and that led to depression and anxiety.

But when he was in the eighth grade, he just couldn't take it anymore, and he decided to tell his mother what was happening. His mother tried telling the other student's parents about what was going on, but they downplayed it like it was just kids being kids, and the police did the same thing. Lemuel desperately wanted out of that school. He couldn't even walk into the bathroom after what had happened. An anger built up inside of him against the individual who abused him. *How could God allow this to happen to me, especially at a Christian school?* Lemuel would ask himself.

His family ended up moving again, and this time he was placed into a public middle school. He started living a worldly lifestyle and abandoned his faith in God. He got into several fights at school, and in high school, he turned to drugs and unhealthy relationships with girls. While this was happening, Lemuel was still attending church on Sundays and trying to act like a "good Christian." But he was hurting deep inside, and he started feeling suicidal. He hated God, and he hated Christians.

A friend of his had a brother who died by suicide. This friend suggested that Lemuel get out of the state and go to a survival retreat to give God another chance in his life. Lemuel decided to attend the retreat, and it turned out that it wasn't the fun, camping adventure he thought it was going to be. Instead, it was like a very intensive boot camp. The whole experience was better than he could have imagined. Through the physical and emotional challenges of the camp, Lemuel reached his breaking point and reestablished his relationship with God. He was now excited to tell everyone in his life about Jesus, and that was what he planned to do his sophomore year of high school.

He started a Jesus Club at his school. As he ministered to students in school, the teachers and the principal intervened, telling him to stop. He got bullied by other students, but in Lemuel's mind, it was all worth it. Dozens of students came to the Jesus Club, and many gave their lives to the Lord.

Through the painful experiences Lemuel went through in his life, God was able to show him how desperate his generation was. They were trying drugs, sex, dark lifestyles, and other forms of escape in search of something to satisfy them. Lemuel now knew what satisfied the heart because he had made that search in his own life, and he wanted to share what he had learned with anyone he came across.

Wise Counsel and Biblical Insight

God Can Redeem Anyone

Therapist Kim DeBerge says it is common for victims of abuse like the kind Lemuel experienced to blame themselves for what happened to them. "I would say 99 percent of the victims, 99.9 percent of the victims, are still self-blaming," Kim said. "Even though our culture will say, 'It's not your fault,' they're still thinking, *What did I do to cause this to happen to me?*"

We Are Broken but Not Worthless

Although Lemuel experienced terrible abuse as a young student in a Christian school, with the help of God and good friends in his life, he was still able to overcome thoughts of depression, anxiety, anger, and suicide. After turning his life back toward God, Lemuel was empowered to share Christ with others in a very powerful way.

God Is Our Shepherd Who Oversees Our Souls

"The Lord is a refuge for the oppressed, a stronghold in times of trouble. Those who know your name trust in you, for you, Lord, have never forsaken those who seek you" (Psalm 9:9–10 NIV).

PRAYER

Dear Lord, my past experiences with abuse haunt me all the time, and I don't know how to get out of this rut. I feel worthless and dirty because of what I experienced even though it wasn't my fault. Please show me your love for me and show me your plan for my life. Amen.

Day 15

ADOPTING MENTAL ILLNESS

Kelly and her husband had dreams of raising children in a Christian home. They discovered how kids in the foster care system were often orphans who didn't have families. The Lord led them to think of it this way: *We have a family, and there are kids who need families. If not us, then who?*

So, the journey began for Kelly as she opened up her home and adopted four children who were in foster care in Hawaii. Soon after the adoption, she learned that three of her children had very severe mental illnesses. She and her husband didn't know much about mental illness at the time although they expected the kids to have some trauma from being in foster care. They thought they were prepared for that trauma, but they had no idea what they were really in for. The journey with their foster kids became much more excruciating than they could have imagined.

For years afterward, Kelly and her husband had to address issues in their children such as anxiety, depression, bipolar disorder, and suicidal thoughts. Medicine, psychologists, and psychiatric hospitals became the norm. Kelly also realized that her dreams and expectations of the kind of family she imagined were never going to be reality.

When it came to church, Kelly felt isolated because she was afraid of the stigma attached to the mental illness that her kids were going through. She would see other families at church, and things seemed so much better for them. She even became bitter at times. *This can't be my life. This can't be my life. How can this be my life?* she would tell herself. These thoughts felt like a big weight on her, and some mornings she couldn't even get out of bed.

She wanted to fix her kids, to make them better, but as the years went on, she realized she ultimately couldn't do anything about it. However, she never stopped advocating for them and loving them. That's all she could do.

A huge turnaround for Kelly happened when God began teaching her gratitude. Kelly started to see the blessings she had in her life, and that revolutionized her world.

God was able to use Kelly and her painful experiences with her family to help countless other families. Kelly and her husband lived on a ranch in Colorado Springs. They had a love for horses, and they discovered the therapeutic effect of being around these magnificent animals. Her family extended invitations to local teen homeless shelters. Many of the kids who came for a day at the ranch came from adoptive families themselves. She quickly saw the positive impact her eighteen horses were having on kids with mental illnesses, and she was led to make it a ministry.

Kelly would go on to become the founder and executive director of the Flying Horse Foundation, an organization that provides free equine services to at-risk children to help them understand how much they are loved by God. She also took what she learned from her own family and became a nationally recognized child advocate. She spent more than ten years working for Focus on the Family, most recently as its Vice President of Advocacy for Children. She has testified before Congress about the foster care and adoption systems and is the author of the book *Wait No More*.[3]

Kelly was key in helping the state of Hawaii, the same state she adopted her children from, to change their laws to better protect minors from adult exploitation. At that time, she was appointed by Hawaii's governor to serve on the Hawaii Children's Trust Fund, where she became its chair-elect before moving with her family to Colorado.

Wise Counsel and Biblical Insight

Mental Illness Causes Traumas in Families

Recovery coach Pam Lanhart says people living with a family member who suffers from mental illness can experience great trauma. "There's a lot of grief and loss when someone hasn't physically died *but is gone in some other way*. They might be missing, they might be exploited, they might be on the streets and not getting help because of their mental illness," Lanhart said. "Death is just one kind of loss, but there are a lot of other losses. And so, when someone dies, it's easy to run to their loved ones and think, *Okay, they need support. They need help*. However, when someone is experiencing significant trauma or grief because of a loved one's illness, not an actual death, people are less sure how to help. So there's loss and there's pain and

---

3   Kelly and John Rosati, *Wait No More: One Family's Amazing Adoption Journey* (Carol Stream, IL: Tyndale House Publishers, Inc., 2011).

there's suffering and there's trauma, but it's not clearly identified like when someone has died."

Our Expectations Are Not Always God's Expectations

Sometimes we envision the kind of life that we want and expect for ourselves, like Kelly did for her own life. She dreamed of having the "perfect Christian family" and got something completely different. Her life was full of pain and many obstacles as she cared for her adopted children who struggled with severe mental illnesses. However, God led her down a path that resulted in her making a real difference in the lives of many children and their families.

God Gives Peace Even in Times of Chaos

"Do not be anxious about anything, but in every situation, by prayer and petition, with thanksgiving, present your requests to God. And the peace of God, which transcends all understanding, will guard your hearts and your minds in Christ Jesus" (Philippians 4:6–7 NIV).

PRAYER

Dear Lord, I am grieving the loss of the life I wanted for myself, but I know you have a plan for me that I might not realize just yet. Please fill my heart with gratitude and show me your blessings and love. Amen.

Day 16

FROM DREAM
TO NIGHTMARE

Nancy grew up in the Catholic church and went to church every Sunday with her family. She had two older brothers and a younger sister. They were your typical suburban family. Nancy dreamed of meeting her future husband, and when that dream came true and they got married, she dreamed of having children and a house with a white picket fence.

Her dream seemed to be coming true. However, not everything went according to plan. Nancy really wanted to be a mother. She and her husband tried to have children for ten years with no success. They went through many medical procedures, and none of them helped. This was hard on Nancy because she really wanted a family, but she resolved to accept whatever God's will was for her and her husband.

Shortly after that, Nancy found out she was pregnant with a boy. She was overjoyed after trying for so long and was filled with love after giving birth to her first son, Jacob. When Jacob was only three months old, Nancy found out she was pregnant again with another boy. They named him Matthew. Having two sons, and having one so soon after the other, was a huge blessing for Nancy, and she thought she was finally living the dream she wished for.

However, as Jacob grew, his parents started to realize that he was not developing at the rate that was typical for his age. After visiting pediatricians and doctors who could find nothing wrong with him, they concluded that things would eventually be fine with him and that his development would catch up. But he never did.

When Jacob was two-and-a-half years old, Nancy and her husband finally received a medical opinion that something was not right, but it was not clear what the problem was. Jacob was still not walking or talking. When he turned five years old, Nancy started to work with Jacob using sign language in order to communicate. Nancy's other son, Matthew, had no developmental delays, but he also refused to speak much. Matthew saw the way his older brother communicated, and he mirrored Jacob's actions. The two would sit happily and sign with each other all day long.

By the time Jacob started school, his behavior problems started to arise. He would get frustrated and angry with his peers. With an IQ of 47, it started to become clear that Jacob would act like a five-year-old for the rest of his life. However, Jacob understood that there was something different about him compared to other kids his age. Jacob would lash out and even become violent when he reached the age of fourteen.

Nancy didn't know where to look for support. She didn't know any other families going through the same issues. She and her boy felt like oddballs compared to others. Those were very dark days for Nancy as she looked everywhere for some kind of support.

Going to church with Jacob did not seem like an option because of his behavior. So, the family just ended up staying home on Sundays, feeling more and more isolated. It was hard to take Jacob out in public places. He was just naturally loud when he spoke. When he did try to speak, it always turned people's heads, and they would stare or make comments. After a while, Nancy became pretty thick-skinned and acted like it did not seem to bother her. She just got used to it. However, she started to feel more alone in her struggles as a mother of a special needs child. That anxiety led to a lack of sleep at night.

The extra time required to parent Jacob meant that there was less time to respond to Matthews needs. Although Nancy and her husband did their best to divide everything evenly between Jacob and Matthew, it was clear that Jacob demanded the most attention. Matthew was forced to be patient at times, and although it appeared that Matthew was handling it just fine, it would become apparent later that the family's struggles had an effect on him.

Matthew was developing at a normal rate, and by the time Jacob was five years old, his younger brother was out-growing him. Matthew quickly became more mature as Jacob remained in a younger state of mind, but those early influences had affected Matthew's emotional development. By the time he was a teenager, it was obvious that something was going on with him. He was internalizing all his emotions until they erupted like a volcano.

As a young teen, Matthew was diagnosed with depression, and tragically, he would turn to drugs and alcohol. He visited multiple treatment centers throughout his teenage years, but his addiction kept growing worse. By the time he was eighteen, he was consistently using meth, and his behavior became erratic.

Nancy's family was crumbling. Her dream was now a nightmare, and she felt like she was losing Matthew. Things with Matthew got so bad that eventually Nancy had to tell her son that if he continued using drugs, he would no longer be able to live in their home. They even had a family contract where Nancy could randomly drug test Matthew, and if he tested positive, she could make him leave.

When Matthew's drug test revealed he had meth in his system five days before Christmas, Nancy did not want to tell him to leave on a holiday. But she knew she had to. Matthew stayed at a homeless shelter and soon became hooked on heroin. After he had been gone for over a month, Matthew finally called his mom out of the blue and told her that he had overdosed and was on his way to the hospital. She learned that he had tried to commit suicide. He was still only eighteen.

Nancy finally broke down and cried out to God. She and her husband had no more energy left to take care of their son with special needs and had no answers for their other son who was out of control. Nancy didn't see how she could keep going, let alone recapture the dream she had lost. She finally found a support group and completely surrendered to God. There, she met families in very similar situations. After attending meetings for a few weeks and praying with other struggling parents, she finally had some sort of hope. She found a new love for her children, no matter where they were in life, and a new appreciation for them.

With support from others and little acts of kindness toward her and her family, Nancy has become an advocate for parents with special needs kids or kids with addictions.

Although society is often judgmental toward families struggling in those areas, Nancy knows that showing love and compassion, the same that God shows, is the best way to support others.

Wise Counsel and Biblical Insight

Todd Mulliken

Nancy's journey involved a lot of years of just surviving. Whether it was the decade-long pain of infertility or the parenting of two children with significant intellectual and emotional challenges, life was incredibly stressful and isolating. But in her darkest hour, after Matthew tried to take his life, she yielded to her Creator. She allowed God to do what she couldn't.

Through her connection with a life-changing support group, she found community. She found hope. This helped her reframe her view of her children. She started to see them as God sees them. With these changes, along with advocating for others who are in similar situations, her life is now forever transformed. She is now thriving instead of simply surviving.

God Will Show You the Way When You Can't See a Path Forward: Suggested Scripture from Pastor Paul Johnson

"For this reason, ever since I heard about your faith in the Lord Jesus and your love for all God's people, I have not stopped giving thanks for you, remembering you in my prayers. I keep asking that the God of our Lord Jesus Christ, the glorious Father, may give you the Spirit of wisdom and revelation, so that you may know him better. I pray that the eyes of your heart may be enlightened in order that you may know the hope to which he has called you, the riches of his glorious inheritance in his holy people, and his incomparably great power for us who believe. That power is the same as the mighty strength he exerted when he raised Christ from the dead and seated him at his right hand in the heavenly realms" (Ephesians 1:15–20 NIV).

PRAYER

My dear God, life is not turning out like I thought it would. Though I have tried hard while following my hopes and dreams, now it seems that everything is falling apart. I turn to you, acknowledging my weakness and my inability to steer the future. You have a better plan. You have promised that you will light the way. I give all my confusion, pain, and darkness to you. Please make something beautiful from it. Amen.

Section 6

LOSS OF
INNOCENCE

Day 17

GOOD FROM EVIL

Scott experienced incest when he was seven at the hands of a family member who was twice his age. This abuse occurred in various places in the home, ranging from bathrooms to closets. These activities led Scott to become interested in other sexual topics, such as pornography, which a neighbor introduced to him. He also discovered masturbation at an early age.

Even at a young age, he knew the older family member's actions were wrong, but he kept the abuse a secret from his parents for ten years. He grew up in a Christian family that was involved in ministry, and that made him feel even more shame and guilt about his secret.

Scott fell into sexual addiction as he entered middle school. When he turned seventeen years old, he finally told his mother about the incest that had been going on, and he even confronted his abusive family member about it. But that didn't stop his sex addiction.

Now in Bible college, Scott even opened up about his sexual addiction to other people, seeking some kind of support. However, just about everyone he talked to was also struggling with the same issues. For the next thirteen years, he was unable to find the support and help he needed to overcome his addiction. He went on to attend seminary. The school had a computer room, which was new at the time. It was there where he discovered internet pornography. This sent Scott deeper and deeper into bondage.

After seminary, Scott worked at a church for a while but quit that and started using his undergrad training in music education to teach music at a public school for a number of years. He reentered the ministry, and he finally found a recovery program for his sexual addiction in his early thirties. Meeting other men who had the same struggles but who had actually overcome them was the first thing that helped Scott make real progress. Memorizing Scripture as a way to get truth deep inside him was also a big help for Scott. "Yet you desired faithfulness even in the womb; you taught me wisdom in that secret place" (Psalm 51:6 NIV).

God was working on Scott and prepping him for his future wife, who had dated him and broken up with him twice earlier. She moved out to Colorado, and they hadn't talked in five years. She reentered his life just before he went into recovery, and they would go on to get married.

As Scott got older and recalled the abuse in his past, it was painful to think about. He now realized how the loss of innocence at an early age led to his struggles with pornography. But God still found a use for that life experience to draw Scott closer to him. Scott now has the experience and knowledge to help others who are struggling with past sexual abuse at the hands of family members and powerful sexual addictions.

Wise Counsel and Biblical Insight

Sexual Bondage Brings Shame

Jessica Teresi, an advocate for sexual abuse survivors, explains that victims of sexual abuse don't talk about it, especially something along the lines of incest, like Scott experienced as a young child. "There's a lot of shame when it comes to sexuality," Jessica said. "So, being able to talk with another victim who experienced something like that, about the things we don't like to talk about, is really comforting and can provide a space for healing and understanding."

God Is Always Capable

Scott never could have imagined what good, if any, could come from his dark and shameful past, which started as a victim of incest and led to a life full of pornography and sexual addiction. God was able to transform Scott into someone who understands these issues in a new light and can now help other men who struggle with sexual addiction.

Break Free of Bondage

"It is for freedom that Christ has set us free. Stand firm, then, and do not let yourselves be burdened again by a yoke of slavery" (Galatians 5:1 NIV).

PRAYER

Dear Lord, I am in bondage to my sexual sin, and no matter what I do, I cannot escape it. Some of this may have started with trauma in my childhood. If that is the case, please heal me from that trauma. I know you want me to be free of this, and I trust that you will help be break the chains of sexual bondage. Amen.

Day 18

ONLY ONE LABEL

Heidi was on her way to a successful life. She grew up in a Christian home and had a good upbringing. She did well in school and excelled in college. So, how did she find herself in a dark world of prostitution and drug addiction?

Heidi was raised on a farm in a small town. Her parents where very loving to her and took her to church. She attended youth group, which she loved. Her father went to Bible college to become a pastor, and her family ended up moving many times. In school, she got straight *A*s, but the constant moving was hard for her. She was in a different school almost every year in high school, and making friends was tougher with each move. She became a little resentful and began rebelling as a senior.

Heidi graduated in the top five of her class and received a full four-year Air Force ROTC scholarship. But that rebellious life followed her to college. She carried some anger at God and her parents. She lost the strong foundation she had in her church. Heidi started drinking more and going to pimp bars, where pimps came looking to trade girls and girls came looking for pimps. It became easier to take more risks, and that led to her losing her virginity, sadly, from rape. She eventually moved in with a man who was a pimp.

The man was fifteen years older than Heidi, and he was a brutal man and very abusive. They eventually got married, and when she got pregnant, she was afraid to bring a child into that world. She had an abortion because she had no one to turn to. She thought of going back home, but her family was moving out of the country to be missionaries.

Heidi became a stripper and worked in escort services. Her husband made her move out to Los Angeles with him, and that is where she started working as a prostitute. She began using drugs and endured rapes, beatings, and pistol whippings. It got so bad that she struggled to escape that life a couple times by running away from her husband, but she would find herself coming back to him. She became pregnant again, and after Heidi had her son, her husband would use the child as leverage, threatening to take him away from her if she ever tried to leave.

By that time, her parents had returned to pastor a church in the States. They had no idea if Heidi was dead or alive since she had disappeared from their lives years earlier. As soon as the opportunity presented itself, Heidi was finally able to leave Los Angeles with her child and returned to her family and their church. She had just left a life of extreme drug use and abuse. As a result, she brought a lot of shame and guilt with her as she reentered the church.

Unfortunately, Heidi had not completely escaped her old life, and she soon returned to her abusive relationship and got back into stripping. However, when she got pregnant with her second child, she told herself she couldn't live this way anymore. She asked God for forgiveness, and she received help from an advocate for domestic violence victims.

She gathered her children, left her husband, went back to college, and got her degree. Her ex-husband searched for her and threatened to kill her. Heidi took her children and entered a domestic violence shelter. With their protection and help, she finally got away from him. While in the shelter, Heidi began doing advocacy for other victims of domestic violence and started working with women in prostitution to help them find a way out. Although prostitution and that dangerous lifestyle was behind her, Heidi still struggled with an alcohol addiction. She went in and out of recovery.

She claimed to be a Christian, but she wasn't seeing any fruit in her life. As part of her recovery process Heidi entered a time of deep prayer. This experience gave her clarity to see herself as God sees her and helped her to erase all the labels she had taken on: victim, survivor, damaged, dirty. God released the victim mentality from her so she could make real strides in her life. Heidi is now sober and lives near her son, daughter-in-law, and grandkids. She has been given a second chance in life. Her new identity is in Christ.

Wise Counsel and Biblical Insight

Anyone Can Be Redeemed by God

As an advocate for sexual abuse survivors, Jessica Teresi says anyone can receive healing from their past, no matter what. "Being free to just be honest with yourself in that process, accepting Jesus and loving God, especially as a trauma victim is really hard to do for some people," Jessica says. "Instead of being frustrated or even jealous that maybe your walk with Jesus doesn't look like the walk of the other people in your life, remember that you have a very special and specific relationship with him, and it is through your personal struggles, it is through your private tribulations, that you are going to be able to have such a stronger bond when you come to understand who he is in your life and how he helps you in hearing his voice."

God Never Gives Up on Us

Heidi went astray from her church and family and found herself in a dark and dangerous place in her life. Even after Heidi lived twelve years of prostitution, rape, abuse, and drug addiction, God never discarded her, but when she was ready for a real change, he opened doors for her to have the chance for a fulfilling and meaningful life.

God Is Our Shepherd Who Oversees Our Souls

"For 'you were like sheep going astray,' but now you have returned to the Shepherd and Overseer of your souls" (1 Peter 2:25 NIV).

PRAYER

Dear Lord, I have gone astray from you. I have been in some very dark places and experienced some terrible things. I feel shameful and guilty before you. I know those feelings don't come from you. Please shower me with your love and forgiveness and reveal to me your purpose for my life. Amen.

Day 19

NEW LIFE IN PRISON

Gina and her daughter, Danielle, held a book together as the two-year-old struggled to pronounce some of the words. Gina was trying to teach her daughter how to appreciate books while she had the opportunity to spend some time with her in the visiting room. Eventually the guard came and told her visiting time was almost up and that she would soon have to go back to her cell. Gina was serving time for a felony conviction, but luckily, the prison allowed her to spend some special time with her child. Every day she would ask herself, *How did things get this bad?* She wondered if she would ever get a second chance.

Gina started using drugs when she was thirteen years old. It started with smoking weed and then using meth in the seventh grade. When she was fifteen, she started hanging out with adults, and she felt cool doing it. That led to sleeping with older men, but she felt grown up and mature enough to make those decisions.

At sixteen, she went to jail for the first time for auto theft. At that time, she had been a runaway for three months. While still young, she already knew her life was a mess. After her release from jail, she went back to high school, but the same pattern continued. She would skip school, run away, sell drugs, and get high.

She had her first child, Danielle, at age nineteen, and she was arrested for her first felony at twenty. Gina was at a friend's place smoking weed when the drug task force raided the house and found a large amount of cocaine. Gina was eventually charged with a felony, and after attempting treatment and violating probation, the judge ordered her to be sent to prison.

After her release from prison, Gina moved in with her parents and enrolled in school. She tried to do the right thing, but she wanted community around her, whether it was good or bad. She ended up right back among the negative influences and bad relationships that all led to trouble.

Gina was never satisfied with her weight, and drugs were a way of helping with that. She wanted to be physically attractive, like the women she saw in magazines and on TV. Meth use caused her to lose a lot of weight very quickly. Eventually, Gina faced her fourth drug charge and another charge for a credit card crime. She was looking at serving more time in prison.

While she was sixth months pregnant with her third child, she was in a high-speed police chase and nearly killed herself and her unborn child in a crash. A correctional officer asked her what she was going to do with this child when it was born, and that question forced Gina to start thinking seriously about her life.

While in jail, she worked with an adoption agency and found a family for her unborn son. For the first time, she was thinking about someone else rather than herself. She wanted her son to have the best life possible even if she didn't get another chance. Gina felt like the beginning of the end was near. She was not only losing her unborn child, but now she was forced to put her other two children up for adoption as well: her eight-year-old daughter and two-year-old son. It was a heartbreaking experience.

Gina had eleven more years to serve in prison, and she wanted to use them in the best way she could in hopes that she could develop relationships with her kids when she got out. She did everything she could to cut her time in prison, including attending a Bible class.

She read Jeremiah 29:11 and learned that God knew the plans for her life, plans to prosper and hope for a future. At first, Gina didn't believe the verse applied to her after everything that had happened. She felt like religion was just a crutch for those in prison, and she didn't want much to do with God. By the end of the class, she was amazed at the belief others had in Jesus. She even admired their faith. Deep down inside, she just wanted what they had, so she talked to a Bible study instructor. The instructor told Gina to pray and ask God to reveal himself to her. Gina tried praying for the first time, not knowing what to expect.

On the following Mother's Day, Gina called her mom. She got the surprise of a lifetime when her mother told her that Gina's kids were back home. After ten months of parenting Gina's kids, the adoptive family decided that it was not God's plan for them. At that moment, in the tiny phone room in her prison, Gina's heart broke. She now knew that God had broken her heart and filled her with his spirit and a new identity. She had read in 1 Corinthians that she would be a new creation in Christ with the old things gone away and the new things to come (1 Corinthians 5:17). For the first time in her life, she finally believed she was worth a second chance.

After her last stint in prison, Gina turned her life around for good. She now works with one the largest treatment programs in her state, Minnesota Adult and Teen Challenge, as director of advocacy. She has also conducted trainings with law enforcement officials and judges, along with attorneys and prosecutors, on the value of second chances. Gina was also an instrumental part of an historical movement for sentencing reform in her state.

Gina is now married, and her children and grandchildren are a big part of her life. She is now convinced that her life is proof that God can repair any situation, no matter how messed up it is.

Wise Counsel and Biblical Insight

Flipping the Script: Advice from Counselor Todd Mulliken

Gina's story demonstrates how difficult it is to cope with the internal pain of having low self-esteem complicated by drug use. Gina's moments of clarity throughout her drug addiction gave her windows of hope, albeit momentarily. Ultimately, her exposure to faith and other people whose authentic desire was to depend on God for their next choice was transformational. Her capacity to look outside herself, to put others ahead of herself, and know that she was loved by God was a game changer!

God Will Never Give Up on You: Suggested Scripture from Pastor Paul Johnson

"Be strong and courageous. Do not be afraid or terrified because of them, for the Lord your God goes with you; he will never leave you nor forsake you" (Deuteronomy 31:6 NIV).

God Will Rescue You from the Fires of Life: Suggested Scripture from Pastor Paul Johnson

"If we are thrown into the blazing furnace, the God we serve is able to deliver us from it, and he will deliver us from Your Majesty's hand. But even if he does not, we want you to know, Your Majesty, that we will not serve your gods or worship the image of gold you have set up" (Daniel 3:17–18 NIV).

PRAYER

Dear Lord, thank you for your redemptive acts that continually amaze me. You never give up on me, even when I've given up on myself. You are a wonderful and gracious God. I am never beyond your reach. You are my only hope. Amen.

Day 20

GOD TOOK A FELON

Sara listened intently to the woman speaking. The prison that she was in allowed a guest speaker to come and share her own story of incarceration and rehabilitation. For the first time in years, Sara had hope. The eight-time felon had hit rock bottom and was facing nine years for a new charge that surfaced only days before her release date.

Sara grew up in a typical suburban household. When she was in the third grade, her mother had a stillborn baby boy and that sent her mom into major depression. Her mother began neglecting Sara at an early age, and eventually Sara's mother ended up in a psych ward.

Sara began acting out, and that landed her in juvenile detention centers for running away from home. At the age of twelve, she was using marijuana and alcohol. By the time she was fifteen, she was out of control. About the same time, her mother was diagnosed with breast cancer. Life was a mess.

It was at this time when Sara met her future husband. Sara and her husband would have two daughters, but marriage and family did nothing to clean up her mess, and there was no fairy-tale ending. The relationship with her husband became very abusive.

Not long after Sara's children were born, her mother passed away. With the loss of her mother, combined with her husband's abuse, Sara turned to crack cocaine and other drugs as a source of comfort. Three short months later, she lost custody of her kids. She decided to just leave home.

Sara left Arizona and started driving to North Carolina. After driving 1,800 miles with no sleep, she totaled her car in Nashville, Tennessee. Officers asked her where she was going. She said she didn't know. She didn't know anything. They gave her a voucher to a homeless shelter there, which was located right by the prostitution strip. She was introduced to that lifestyle, and she became a prostitute, which only helped her earn money to get more drugs.

She would live this way for the next twelve years. Sara was in and out of jail and rehabilitation centers, and it was all just one big cycle. Sara had opportunities to reach out to friends or other people for support, but her desire for drugs kept her chained in her bad habits. It wasn't until she had been sitting in prison for seven years and was getting ready to get out to go to boot camp, a minimum-security program that teaches cognitive skills along with physical training in order to help reduce incarceration time. She was excited because, to her, that meant she could get out and get high again.

However, God had a different plan. Two weeks before her release, another charge showed up against her, and now she was looking at another nine years in prison. Without drugs to cope, Sara was in mental torment. She could not imagine spending nine more years in prison.

Then a guest speaker showed up at her prison, someone with a very similar story, only the speaker's story ended with the promise of redemption. Sara was so inspired that she finally had *real* hope that she could change and turn her life around. She finally cried out to God. She had nowhere else to go, so she surrendered to him. Sara got baptized in prison and prayed for God to take her desire for drugs away.

It was now time for her to go before the judge to answer for the new charges. Although she was an eight-time felon, which should have resulted in a sentence with no leniency, the judge decided to charge her like she had no previous crimes. She was released six days later on her original release date. After that, she went to Minnesota Adult & Teen Challenge, and God gave her a sound mind and joy that she had never experienced before. Sara was able to reconnect with her daughters after fourteen years of being without them. She went back to school and got an education and a degree so she could work as an addiction counselor. She now has two grandchildren and a life she could never have imagine before.

Wise Counsel and Biblical Insight

God Can Make Our Lives Beautiful No Matter What

Sara had a very ugly past, but God never gave up on her and restored relationships, friends, and family in her life. God took what was bad in her life and turned it into something good as Sara is now an addiction counselor helping others who have struggled with the same things she once did.

God Grants Peace to Us Even during the Chaos

"When you were dead in your sins and in the uncircumcision of your flesh, God made you alive with Christ. He forgave us all our sins, having canceled the charge of our legal indebtedness, which stood against us and condemned us; he has taken it away, nailing it to the cross" (Colossians 2:13–14 NIV).

PRAYER

Dear Lord, I am grieving the loss of my childhood and innocence. My past is full of ugliness. Please turn my life around into something beautiful that will serve others and that is pleasing to you. Amen.

Day 21

GOD LOVES ME NO MATTER WHAT I'VE DONE

KJ's parents divorced when she was only four years old. After the divorce, her mother started drinking heavily and, in a short time, became an alcoholic.

At an early age, Kjersti was exposed to many things a child should never see. She saw pornography and strange men coming in and out of her house. She found out later that this was the way her mother made money to pay the bills. It didn't take long for Kjersti to learn that it was better for her to stay out of the picture so her mother could do what she did. That led to her being neglected by her mother. She was even sexually abused by some of the men who came to their house.

When KJ was eight years old, she and her mother moved into her mother's boyfriend's house. He was a heavy drinker, and both he and her mother would visit the bar frequently. Her mother ended up marrying the man, so he became KJ's stepfather.

KJ became very involved at school. She was on the cheerleading squad, a homecoming candidate, and was on the student council. However, at thirteen years old, she started using drugs, became very promiscuous, and started hanging out with kids who were a bad influence on her. She just seemed to click with other kids who also had parents who were not around much.

By age fourteen, KJ was spending time at the same bar her mom frequented. Inappropriate behavior, patrons getting drunk, and suggestive comments were the norm. One day after school, when KJ was still a freshman, her life took a turn for the worse when two male friends from school offered to give her a ride home but ended up driving her to a vacant parking lot and raping her. Even though her mother found out about it, she really didn't seem to care.

KJ became friends with another girl who introduced her to a strip club that was hiring. At first, Kjersti could never see herself working there. But, when she turned eighteen, she didn't think she had anything to lose, so she gave it a shot. When she went in, the manager looked her up and down and said she could make a lot of money there.

The first couple of times she worked there, it was almost too embarrassing for her. But when she saw how much money she was making, the embarrassment started to go away, and she became less afraid. Eventually, she embraced what she was doing. Additionally, working at the strip club provided KJ with an unlimited supply of drugs. Her cliental included men who worked at her school and even her vice principal. Her mom's friends would come in as well as her friends from high school.

KJ was now a daily drug user. One day she and her friends got high and then went to a movie. During the movie, one of the characters said, "Remember who you are." For some reason, that stuck with KJ, and God shattered her heart in that moment. For so long, she tried to find her identity, and deep down inside, she knew being a stripper was not who she really was.

God filled her with his spirit, and she had a newfound hope. She decided to quit working in the strip club and go back to school to become a teacher. She started reading a Bible her stepmother had given to her, and she had a completely new understanding of God, but she hadn't yet given her life to him.

In college, KJ met a guy, and they ended up getting married. But she was still drinking and using drugs, and things got worse when she had an affair. She was terrified because she did not want to take the responsibility for her actions, so she ran away from her husband. She went back to working in the strip club, but it didn't last long. KJ did not want to be there, and she broke down and called her husband, saying she wanted to come back home.

A year later, she got sober and divorced her husband. She got married a second time, and they had a daughter. She finally invited Jesus into her life, and things began to change. She joined an online church that helps people who struggle with pornography, and she started her own survivor-led outreach program to minister to women in strip clubs. She now has a deep passion for helping women in the sex industry, and she works to help them know that Jesus loves them no matter what.

KJ began journaling and writing about her experiences and her life. She would go on to publish a book about her life and the dark world of the sex industry. It took many years for KJ to surrender, but God took hold of KJ to show her how valuable she really is, no matter what she had done or experienced.

Wise Counsel and Biblical Insight

God Is Desperate to Be Close to You

In Luke 15, Jesus tells three stories to demonstrate his passionate desire to be close to you. In fact, the less worthy you feel, the more he presses in to find you. In each gospel story, God shows how he won't stop pursuing you but wants to give you the power to choose him. Let this be the moment you draw closer to the God who is waiting to be close to you.

God Deeply Values Emotion and Honors Pain

In Psalm 51:17, the author, David, reveals what God most treasures in all the universe, even above all the wonders around us. He writes, "My sacrifice, O God, is a broken spirit; a broken and contrite heart you, God, will not despise." A broken heart, a hurt spirit, is something more valuable to God than anything else that we can offer to him.

The More Broken You Are, the More Powerful You Become

In Ephesians 2:10, Paul describes you as "God's workmanship," a beautifully crafted and precious piece of art. The more hurt and brokenness you have experienced, the more qualified you are to relate to those who are lost. If you have been truly broken and lost, then you have a deeper understanding of what it's like to need to be found. Just like KJ, who now has the powerful ability to reach those lost in the adult sex industry, your pain and suffering provide you with the power to reach people others cannot. Spend time today meditating on the idea of the power you now bring to the mission to rescue others.

PRAYER

Lord, God, the one so desperate to draw near to each of us, may we see ourselves as you see us: the unique piece of artwork specifically designed to draw near to you and to seek others. I pray each of us would have our spiritual eyes opened to the value we each possess and the healing that comes from knowing the God who will not stop pursuing a relationship with us. And show us whom we are specifically designed to reach, a position hard earned from our life's pain. Amen.

TRAFFICKED, ADDICTED, CHILDREN LOST. GOD RESTORES

Growing up, Jennifer's family seemed mostly normal. She was raised in a middle-class family and lived in the suburbs. Her mother was very creative and played the guitar. Sometimes, Jennifer found herself sitting at the top of the stairs listening to her mother play and sing. Jennifer and her siblings were allowed to read or play outside, but they were not allowed to watch TV or stay up late. They had an 8:00 p.m. bedtime. Jennifer felt that these and some of the other rules set by her mother seemed too strict, and she became angry with her mother.

Despite the rules, Jennifer knew her mother loved her. She knew this because her father cheated on her mother, and even after finding out, her mother never said anything negative about her father to the kids. Even when he moved out, Jennifer's mother wanted them to know that their faither loved them.

Jennifer's mother was very wholesome, but her father liked promiscuous women. Jennifer wanted to be loved, and because of the kind of women her father liked, she began to believe that being beautiful and attractive to men would bring love in her life. Her self-image and mental health started to spiral out of control, and when she was twelve years old, she made her first suicide attempt.

Her mother started to take Jennifer to behavioral centers and treatment facilities. This made Jennifer even more upset with her mother, so she decided to go live with her father. This meant Jennifer attended a new high school. However, her dad was never home, so eventually she stopped going to class. She met a friend, and they both ran away together.

As a runaway at the age of fourteen, Jennifer was vulnerable, and it was at this time that she met her first human trafficker. He began filling her young mind with ideas that made sense to her at the time. He would tell her that her parents were no good and that he understood her like no one else. He showed her around town and introduced her to prostitutes. At first, she could not find it in herself to do what they did, but that kind of lifestyle became more and more attractive when the other women would show her their fur coats and other things they bought with the money they made.

Jennifer eventually looked up to these women and wanted to be like them. That desire would launch her twenty-eight-year career in prostitution. During that time, she was with four different traffickers. The first one introduced her to prostitution, and the second one, who was a little older, introduced her to drugs. While using cocaine regularly, Jennifer was unaware that she was pregnant with her daughter. When her daughter was born, she had cocaine in her system, and she went into state custody. Over time, Jennifer had three more children, all boys.

The third trafficker took care of Jennifer and even her kids. He would always get her out of jail, drive her to her calls, and protect her from other pimps. However, after a while,

Jennifer started to feel very used. She wanted to get out of the lifestyle, but it almost seemed impossible.

Jennifer attempted suicide a few more times. She was at the point where she hated herself and her life. She had lost her relationships with her three sons, there was no love in her life, and she felt used up. Jennifer decided that suicide was not an option anymore. She would turn to God. She prayed and asked him to take over her life. She didn't know how to make it happen, but she wanted something different. She wanted integrity back. She wanted love back in her life.

She ended up moving into a house, and one of her sons moved in with her with one request: no men around. Jennifer agreed even though she was still working in prostitution. She didn't know how else to make money. But over time, her relationships with her kids and siblings were mending. This motivated her to make even more changes in her life.

Although she had quit drugs entirely, she also wanted to be out of prostitution for good. She asked God to help her find a way to support herself and her children without having to sell herself. The very next day she got a letter in the mail that said she could live in her house for a year without paying rent because it had been foreclosed. She then saw the possibility of living outside of prostitution.

Her family went above and beyond to help her once she was free of prostitution. But things didn't stop there for Jennifer. God had a plan to use her ugly past for something beautiful. Today, Jennifer is a survivor advocate at a non-profit agency that helps women and girls escape systems of prostitution and sexual exploitation through advocacy and education. God has helped her see her true identity as someone who is valued, trusted, wanted, and useful.

Wise Counsel and Biblical Insight

Have you ever thought, *I have sinned so badly that I will never be forgiven*? Jennifer believed that lie. As a retired Marriage, Family, and Child Therapist, Terri Hands heard this many times. But Terri can tell you that it was when Jennifer took that leap of faith and said she would trust Jesus that everything changed for her.

We see the things we do wrong as permanent stains on our lives. Jesus sees them differently. He said to Jennifer, and is saying to you, "I, even I, am he who blots out your transgressions, for my own sake, and remembers your sins no more" (Isaiah 43:25 NIV). Jesus Christ came to earth to *redeem* us. To *redeem* us means that he paid a price for us so that we can be set free from any type of captivity we've been living in. Jesus then makes us into a *new creation*. Through Jesus we become someone different than who we were. "Therefore, if anyone is in Christ, the new creation has come: The old has gone, the new is here!" (2 Corinthians 5:17 NIV).

He gives us a new life by redeeming and restoring all the years that we feel like we have wasted in our lives. Instead, he takes all those years and weaves them into our and his glorious story! Look at Rahab (Joshua 2), who was in a life of prostitution. She had faith and trusted God. "By faith the prostitute Rahab, because she welcomed the spies, was not killed with those who were disobedient" (Hebrews 11:31 NIV). Rahab's past will always be part of our and God's story. She will always be remembered as the mother of Boaz, who was the father of Obed, who was the father of Jesse, who was the father of King David, which ultimately, was the family line of Jesus, who came to redeem all of us.

PRAYER

Dear Lord, I have lived in shame long enough. Thank you for showing me that by trusting in you, I can be forgiven by you and that that old part of my life is behind me. I am a new creation in your image! You came to give me a life of love, joy, and freedom! In your loving, forgiving, redeeming name, amen!

Day 23

AN UNFAIR START, A LIFE OF MEANING, RESTORED FOR ETERNITY

Even though Sheila Raye's father was famous, she never met him when she was a child. She only had memories of her mother struggling to raise her. Singer and songwriter Ray Charles fathered twelve children, and Sheila was one of them, but it didn't mean much to her as a child. Famous or not, her father wasn't there to protect her, and her mother was an alcoholic.

Life turned dark for Sheila at just five years old when she was first molested by her babysitter. The molestation would go on until she was twelve. That left her feeling sad, confused, and angry. This led to a rebellious lifestyle when she became a teenager. Sheila was on her own and struggling to find her own identity.

Sheila finally met her father when she was fourteen, but by then, her life was already on a downward spiral. The molestation from her childhood made her angry and confused, causing her to act out as a teen. She wanted to pay back the world for her pain. She ran away from home, stole things from stores, experimented with drugs, and became as promiscuous as possible. As long as she was not a victim anymore, that's all that mattered.

Her drug addiction started with smoking marijuana, but that led to pills, then crystal meth, and then crack cocaine. Sheila developed a very strong addiction to cocaine and would emerge from a drug-induced haze to find herself in a crack house or some other dark place. She would even steal presents from under the Christmas tree at her family's house and sell them so she could use the money to buy crack.

Sheila would go on to have children of her own, and they were born addicted to crack cocaine. It seemed to Sheila that she could not find her place in the world, even as a mother. She didn't want to be like her own alcoholic mother. Her identity had been ripped away from her at an early age from the molestation she experienced. She felt like she never grew up like a little girl should. That was still very painful for her to think about as an adult. Eventually, all five of her children were taken away from her.

For years, people told her that she would never change, and she gave them a good reason to believe that. The drugs and fast lifestyle landed Sheila in federal prison three times. But during her third stint in prison, Sheila read the Bible, and she felt that God was speaking to her directly. She had finally hit rock bottom, and she had nowhere else to go, so she started with baby steps. First, she was able to forgive herself. Next, she was able to forgive her father and others in her life. In her prison cell, she asked God to fill her with his love, wisdom, and peace. Surrendering her life to God brought her joy she could never imagine.

Once Sheila was released from prison, a judge gave her the chance to see and reconnect with her children, something she thought she would never get to do. She went on to form lasting relationships with most of her children, and she spent as much time as possible with her grandchildren.

Her journey in life gave Sheila a passion for people in prison and for people who have no hope. Later, when Sheila met and married her husband, Tony, they joined One Way Up ministry, which allowed them to go from prison to prison and use their life stories to give others hope and to encourage inmates to improve their lives. They also founded their own non-profit organization to fight against addiction, unjust incarceration, and human trafficking.

Sheila passed away in June of 2017 at the age of fifty-three after a battle with breast cancer. Her life is now fully restored for eternity. We are grateful that she shared her story with us.

Wise Counsel and Biblical Insight

God Offers Us Himself as a Parent

Jesus promises us that regardless of the failings of our earthly fathers, God will not abandon us. In John 14:18, he said to his disciples before physically leaving the earth, "I will not leave you as orphans, I will come to you." What he was promising was to give us his Spirit, whom he called "the Helper" who would walk with us, choosing to feel our pain and suffering, while providing his love and guidance (John 14:16–17).

God Wants to Free Us

Jesus said in John 8:32, "the truth will set you free." The truth he was referring to is the treasure found in his love. If you are literally in prison serving a sentence, emotionally in prison, bound by your past, or facing the pain of both: God longs to free your spirit from the pain it carries. Your past choices do not have to dictate how you view yourself. The whole message of the Bible is built on the idea that God loves freeing people from their past.

You Have a Unique Identity in Him

God has placed his personal divine seal on you, a spiritual mark that signifies that you are his. Paul wrote, "Now it is God who makes both us and you stand firm in Christ. He anointed us, set his seal of ownership on us, and put his Spirit in our hearts as a deposit, guaranteeing what is to come" (2 Corinthians 1:21–22 NIV). Picture your forehead with a beautiful mark, something that represents an identity not in your past but in your present and your future. With that seal, you are given the voice to share with those around you all that he has done for you and in you.

PRAYER

Lord God, give us a picture in our minds of the seal placed on us, the mark that we are no longer what we have done but we are what we have in you: your Spirit, the mark that you have not left us alone but have chosen to walk the road of this painful world. And as we take each step, grounded in knowing that this life is not easy, may we find in your love the basis for our courage to keep going. One step at a time. Amen.

Section 7

LOSS OF
PHYSICAL HEALTH

AN EXPERT IN SUFFERING

Sandy's life started out normal for the most part. She was the youngest of four, and her parents worked hard to support them. Her mom and dad were not overly loving, but they did what they could for their family. Sandy, as the youngest child, learned how to become self-reliant and independent. She began to experiment with alcohol when she was in high school and fell in love with the party lifestyle. On graduation day, she got a DUI.

When it came to love and romance, she looked for it everywhere. However, no matter where she looked, she couldn't find it. The desire to be loved turned into desperation, and that led her to dangerous and dark places. If she did have a relationship with someone, it was only short-lived. The cycle of broken romances left her more hurt and emptier inside.

On October 23, 1984, Sandy was driving her car on a highway and approached a bridge. She noticed in her rearview mirror that a semitruck was weaving in and out of traffic, moving from the left lane to the right lane. She tried to let the truck pass, but when she did so, the truck came over into her lane and hit the front of her car. The trailer of the truck and the cement median on the bridge stopped her car immediately and the momentum forced her car to flip forward. The accident left

Sandy paralyzed from the shoulders down. She was only twenty years old, and life as she knew it came to a crashing end.

While she was in the hospital, Sandy dealt with conflicting emotions as she tried to grapple with what had happened. Before the accident, she had worked in a nursing home as a certified nursing assistant and was keenly aware of what it was like when your body did not function properly.

Why had this happened to her? She was deeply hurt thinking about it. She could not bear the thought of being trapped in her numb body for the rest of her life, having to depend on others for every need. She believed her life had lost all purpose. Those who had been by her side when the accident happened moved on with their lives. Sandy felt stuck and alone. At night, she would ask God to end her life.

Two and a half years after the accident, Sandy's oldest sister invited her to a new church, and she accepted. Sandy grew up attending church but really never had a true relationship with God. She accepted her sister's invitation, and a short time later, she got involved in a Bible study. The Holy Spirit revealed to Sandy that she was a sinner and needed the redemptive grace and mercy offered by Jesus. Up until that point, she had never understood the sacrificial love of Jesus on the cross. Sandy was overcome by the most profound love she had ever experienced, the kind of love she had been searching for her whole life. She gave her heart to Jesus. With this newfound love in her heart, she became more involved at church. She began volunteering any way she could. She answered phone calls, greeted people at the door, and volunteered as a part of the prayer team. She was even a small-group leader for some of the classes.

This is when Satan launched an attack on Sandy by trying to convince her that her quiet nature was the result of her having nothing worthwhile to say. Sandy started to believe this lie and withdrew from social events. Her isolation got worse and worse until she was depressed, and the feelings of worthlessness returned. With the help of friends and prayer, Sandy was able to overcome these feelings and became even more involved in the church. Her life became even more fulfilled with purpose and meaning.

Today, Sandy can look back on her life and see the suffering but also the immense blessings she received from God through those sufferings. God had given her a new and profound perspective on life that many others will never have. When she meets people and they learn about her injuries, many say things like, "I could never live like that." But for Sandy, she wouldn't have it any other way because of how God used the events in her life to bring her to him. She learned that with Jesus, you can overcome any obstacle that you face and that with God, all things are possible. Sandy has become an expert when it comes to the topic of suffering. She can honestly say that her life is better now than what it was before her accident.

There are plenty of Bible verses that deal with suffering, and Sandy has used those to give herself hope and confidence. One of them is Romans 8:18 (NASB), "For I consider that the sufferings of this present time are not worthy to be compared with the glory that is to be revealed to us." For Sandy, this verse comforted her because she realized that no matter how much she suffers with her disability, it does not compare to what lies ahead for her in her new life with Jesus.

Wise Counsel and Biblical Insight

Counselor and Pastor Dan Munson Shares Thoughts on Suffering

In the midst of suffering, sometimes people begin to have doubts and questions, not so much about God and who he is, but why? *Why would these kinds of things happen*? And sometimes the questions come with increasing intensity, to the point where it feels almost unbearable. At those times, what's helpful for me is to come back to the cross, to think about what happened there to Jesus, who was perfect, he had no reason to have anything bad going on in his life, and yet he was murdered for us on a cross. When he was stretched upon that cross, he said, "Father, forgive them," referring to the people who were killing him. He said, "Father, forgive them. They don't know what they're doing" (Luke 23:34 GW). When I can see my suffering in the light of Jesus' suffering, then my doubts and my questions about why God does do that seem to fall into perspective. The question then becomes not so much "Why does God do that?" but "Why does he love me that much?"

Find People Who Will Listen and Share Your Story

When people begin to meet with someone like a therapist, a pastor, or friend, when they truly reach out to share their story with someone, when they share a story of how God brought them through suffering and how they are growing through that, people are often all ears. They want to hear more about that kind of God, the God of love, and to know him even more. They say, "Just hearing your story takes away my need to question *Why, God?* and it makes me want to stop turning away from God."

Suffering Helps Us Know God

Sometimes it takes getting to the end of ourselves, to the end of our own strength, to surrender to our great God. When people are mad at God, facing difficulties with God, they're wanting to know, "Can we believe in God, even while these bad things are happening?" In fact, Sandy says, "My story is that if it wouldn't have been for the difficulties and the hard things that have happened in my life, I would not have known God in such a personal, unique, experiential way. That's what suffering is all about, in my opinion. It brings us to the end of ourselves, to where we begin to be open to communing with our God in such a way that we meet him, for the first time, experientially, not just theologically."

God Can Use Your Suffering

So often, people feel that they've done something wrong to deserve the suffering they are going through. People do make mistakes in life that have consequences, but often it has nothing to do with us. God has something bigger in mind as he is allowing some of the struggles to come. The book of Job is a good illustration. It shows that in the midst of some of those kinds of unfair situations, when Satan thinks we're going to turn away from God, our great God gives us the opportunity to trust in his eternal, absolute, fantastic love to meet us right where we are in those times. A miracle happens at that point, that in the midst of that suffering, our God actually grows us rather than destroying us.

PRAYER

God, help me to resist doubting you. I know that you suffered in ways I can't imagine. When I am feeling sorry for myself and focused on me, help me to see that I am connected to you through suffering and that it helps me know you. Send me people who will listen to me and support me. Help me to see ways that my experiences can be used to help others and to serve you. Amen.

Section 8

LOSS OF
MENTAL HEALTH

Day 25

MAD AT GOD

Margaret had to keep an eye out for her dad…almost daily it seemed. One day he would be happy and fine. Other days he was a completely different person, even cruel at times. Sometimes she would have friends over, and it would be extremely embarrassing to have her dad act the way he did in front of them. He would say things that made no sense at all. She was left in confusion when her dad called an ambulance to come take himself to the hospital.

Now fast-forward a couple of decades. Margaret sat staring at a blank page in a journal during a support group meeting for sexual abuse survivors. She thought about what to write under the question, "What was your reaction when you got abused?" The words flowed out onto the paper effortlessly. *I have to forget this because it's so 'ishy,'* she wrote.

Margaret did not have many memories of her childhood, but with the help of counseling, she was forced to face vague memories of the physical, mental, and sexual abuse she experienced from her father. She learned that her trauma caused her physical problems, even as a child. For example, in the eighth grade, she would throw up every day before school. In the ninth grade, she had high blood pressure. In the tenth grade, she had headaches every day.

Her parents ended up divorcing when she was a junior in high school. She tried to maintain some kind of relationship with her father, but flashes of the abuse caused her to stay away from him. After high school, Margaret went to college and became a nursing assistant. She still carried heavy depression throughout her twenties and into her thirties. But her darkest days occurred in her forties after a special time with her adult children during Easter. After it was over and they left, she felt very low. A back injury added to her difficulties, and some days she felt paralyzed. Her mental health plummeted, and she ended up lying in bed for months. Thoughts of taking her own life crept into her mind. *I could just end this,* she thought to herself. Emotions of anger overwhelmed her as well, and she even found herself cursing at God.

These thoughts lasted for six months. During that time, she lost relationships and friends. She grieved the loss of these relationships, and that sent her into an even deeper depression. But she did have one friend who would still call her every day to check on her and who could relate to her depression. That is where her healing process began.

With the help of a vocational rehabilitation program for her back injury, Margaret started making progress by doing simple jobs and spending less time in bed. God opened up other doors for her, where she learned about deliverance in a new devotional she began reading. She also met a new counselor, who help her envision God differently. For a long time, her vision of God was skewed based on the relationship she had with her father.

Today, church is a huge part of Margaret's life. She still struggles with depression from time to time, but with the support of her counselor, church family, and friends, she is able to see how far God has delivered her from the dark place where she had lived for a long time. The despair of depression and grief of losing friends and relationships was no match for God's love and promise in Margaret's life. Today, she shares that hope with anyone who has experienced what she experienced.

Wise Counsel and Biblical Wisdom

Build a Community around You

Licensed professional counselor Jenita Pace struggled with depression for many years. Now she encourages others who are fighting through this darkness: "If you're going through depression and you continue to struggle, that's not abnormal. We are meant to be in community," she said. "God himself is a Trinity. God isn't even alone. So, if you are out trying to do this independently, understand that you're not meant to do it that way."

Isolation in the Bible

Depression leads to isolation, and even several Bible characters had long bouts of isolation. For example, the prophet Jeremiah dealt with depression and long stretches of isolation. "Cursed be the day I was born! May the day my mother bore me not be blessed!…Why did I ever come out of the womb to see trouble and sorrow and to end my days in shame?" (Jeremiah 20:14, 18 NIV).

God Is Faithful to the Depressed, Even When Others Leave

God is faithful to those with depression and never fails them. "The Lord himself goes before you and will be with you; he will never leave you nor forsake you. Do not be afraid; do not be discouraged" (Deuteronomy 31:8 NIV).

God Intends for Us to Live Joyful Lives

"Rejoice in the Lord always. I will say it again: Rejoice!" (Philippians 4:4 NIV).

PRAYER

Father, I don't know why the bad parts of my story have happened. I don't want to be discouraged but sometimes life is just overwhelming, and I want to hide. Help me to see you in those times. God help me connect with people who will be part of my life and who will help me see the good around me. I know that life will have dark days. Give me courage to face those days and help me take the steps that will bring me closer to your light. Amen.

Day 26

GRIEF IS NOT MY IDENTITY

Growing up, Jessica never envisioned herself being a police officer someday. After high school, she attended college and became a single mom. She entered the ministry working with youth because she had a heart for kids. One fateful day, a friend of hers, who was a police officer, asked her if she wanted to ride along, and she agreed. It didn't take long for her to become intrigued. She went on another ride-along with a different friend from her church who was also a police officer, and that sealed the deal. She knew this was her calling.

Jessica entered the police academy at thirty years old. That's where she met her husband, and they both started their careers at the same time. Getting married meant merging families as Jessica already had a daughter. Jessica and her husband's family grew to three girls in total. Jessica took an early retirement while her husband continued to work as a police officer.

With her early retirement, Jessica started her life as a stay-at-home mom, something she always wanted to do. However, even in her retirement, she continued to use her experience to help train communities on the issue of human trafficking. Everything seemed to be going well for Jessica and her family. People would even ask her what the secret was to her great marriage. But in 2018, everything changed.

That is when she learned about her husband's depression and anxiety. His PTSD from the stress of his job was lurking under the surface for years, and it all came to a head at once. She learned a staggering statistic that more police officers die by committing suicide a year than the number of officers who die in the line of duty or by other means. Her husband's PTSD flipped her whole family upside down. All of a sudden, she was fighting to keep him alive while still taking care of her family.

During the first year of fighting his PTSD, her husband was hospitalized three times. During this time, Jessica didn't tell anyone what was going on with her husband because of the stigma often related to mental health. There was also an additional stigma attached to her family being a law enforcement family. Jessica was already traumatized by all this, and she could not bear to hear negative comments.

The isolation was a self-protective measure for Jessica and her family, but that came at a cost. After a year went by, she realized that she was physically and mentally demolished, and she had to do something. She decided to tell a small group of people at her church what was going on in her family and asked them to pray for her. Later, she concluded that it was a horrible decision. Once she told people at church, they looked at her differently. She was no longer who she used to be in the church, and the same went for her family.

After that, she was usually asked, "How is your husband? Is your husband okay?" She heard these questions Sunday after Sunday. It was all anyone seemed to want to talk to her about. She realized that her identity was gone. Her kids' significance fell away too. It got to a point where Jessica made the decision that she wouldn't return to her church. She just couldn't handle it.

Times for Jessica and her family got very difficult and dark. She was grieving the loss of her husband, who was still alive but not the same man she had married. Her family was in crisis, and her kids seemed lost. Grief, she learned, had no bottom, and just when she thought she couldn't go lower, something would happen and send her even farther down.

When her husband was hospitalized for the fourth time, Jessica didn't pray for a miracle like she did the first three times, but this time she gave her husband over to God, saying he was in God's hands now and to let God's will be done. That was his last hospitalization, and her husband made a huge turnaround. Jessica realized that God was always there with her and her family. She realized that he cares for them and loves them no matter how bad their circumstances get.

Wise Counsel and Biblical Insight

God Is There

Therapist Trisha Vogelsang says no matter how bad things get in our lives, we need to realize that God is always there: "We need to understand we have the power of Jesus in us to take authority over that supernatural demonic and separate it from that which is human. We can shut that door through our time in prayer so that this part is no longer vulnerable. Now, we get to experience inner healing, and we get to invite Jesus into the healing process of those shattered pieces. And he puts us back together. He binds up the brokenhearted. He takes the shattered, broken pieces of our lives, and he puts us back together piece by piece."

God Is Faithful to the Grieving

"Yet this I call to mind and therefore I have hope: Because of the Lord's great love we are not consumed, for his compassions never fail. They are new every morning; great is your faithfulness" (Lamentations 3:21–23 NIV).

Our Identity Is in Christ

Jessica stated that she grieved losing her identity. As a follower of Christ, her true identity never changed. "I have been crucified with Christ and I no longer live, but Christ lives in me. The life I now live in the body, I live by faith in the Son of God, who loved me and gave himself for me" (Galatians 2:20 NIV).

PRAYER

Dear Lord, my heart is heavy with grief, and I feel like I am at my lowest point. Please reveal to me your love and mercy. It seems like no one understands the pain I am feeling. Give me peace of mind and strength to face what lies ahead. Amen.

Day 27

LISTENING TO
HER OWN LIES

Jenita had what most young women wanted. She was a straight A student in college pursuing her career, she had a loving Christian family, and she had just married the love of her life from Bible college. Tim was a very godly young man who wanted to be a pastor.

Yet, something didn't seem right. Everything became very dark and very sad for Jenita. Despite her seemingly perfect life, a deep depression came upon her, and she couldn't understand why. She felt embarrassed because she believed that if you were a Christian, you should be joyful and happy. Also, she was a pastor's wife, and she didn't want others to know what she was going through. She asked Tim to keep her depression private while she tried to figure out what was wrong.

But it just got worse and worse. Jenita started to isolate herself, finding every excuse to be less social with people. She would go to bed and not want to get up the next morning. More and more dark thoughts came into her mind: thoughts that she was holding Tim back and that she was a nuisance to her family, thoughts that they would be better off without her. The lies in her head continued to grow until she decided to take action.

One day, Tim went off to work, and while he was gone, Jenita attempted to take her own life. Amazingly, Tim returned just a few minutes later because he had forgotten something. He discovered that his wife was attempting suicide and quickly took her to the hospital. While she was in the hospital, someone gave her a Bible. She started flipping through it, not looking for anything specifically. She stumbled upon Psalm 121, which talks about the Lord watching over everyone and how he is there to help. When Jenita read that, she felt reassured, and she clung to that verse. While in the hospital, she would read it every hour of the day.

After being released from the hospital, Jenita came home, and several people contacted her. One of them was a professor at her college. He told her that he had been praying for her and he cited Psalm 121. She knew that this was not a coincidence and that God was trying to speak to her.

Then the church where Tim worked wanted to intervene in Jenita's situation. Tim and Jenita were under the impression that the pastor and elders of their church would come to their home and pray for them. However, only the pastor came. Tim and Jenita were very disappointed when the pastor wanted to talk about what sins in Jenita's life had provoked her to attempt suicide. He wanted to see where Jenita was falling short in her faith. The experience with the pastor was terrible, and Tim and Jenita looked for spiritual guidance from others who expressed love toward them rather than judgment.

That is when Jenita became good friends with the wife of the professor who had cited Psalm 121 earlier. Her name was Pat, and she had been in the mission field for years. She had also battled depression when she was overseas and experienced the same kind of rejection from the Christian community over it.

No matter how bad Jenita was feeling, Pat always expressed the same love toward her. While Jenita was in bed and in deep depression, Pat would crawl into bed with her and say, "We can do this." Pat always included herself in Jenita's situation and always used the word *we* as if Pat were on the journey with her. Pat also encouraged Jenita, saying God would use Jenita's depression for good sometime down the road. She would check on Jenita just about every day.

Three weeks after Pat started mentoring Jenita, she had a brain aneurysm and died suddenly. It was very difficult news for Tim and Jenita to hear. The next day, Jenita went to her mailbox and discovered a card that Pat had sent her the day she died. Pat wrote on it, "I want you to write this down so you don't forget that God is going to use this, and I know you don't believe me, but you'll see that I'm right."

That is when Jenita first started feeling some kind of hope. God had a plan for her, even with her depression, that she was not even aware of. Tim and Jenita ended up moving to Minnesota to be closer to Jenita's family. She also entered an outpatient program, and as she worked through the program, she started to realize that she wanted to be a therapist. But then she would snap back into negative thinking and tell herself, *That's a lofty idea.*

But Jenita did just that. She worked hard to get her master's degree in counseling, and she now has her own practice, helping others who are going through what she did. With a fellow therapist, she cowrote a class that uses the analogy of water in the Bible to create concepts that are refreshing to the spirit of someone who's depressed, giving them skills to cope appropriately.

None of this would have been possible without the unconditional love of people like Pat who stood by Jenita the entire time and believed in her no matter how bad her depression became. That love, the same kind of love expressed by Jesus, now helps Jenita to help others who are battling the dark valleys of depression.

Wise Counsel and Biblical Insight

The following is insight from the personal experience of Jenita's husband, Pastor Tim Pace.

Create a Safe Place

One of the most important aspects when dealing with church members who have depression is safety. These people need a safe, welcoming place where they can share their struggles and where they are in life without fear of judgment or rejection. Church staff should be trained to respond to people with generosity and love.

Caregivers Needs Support Too

Don't overlook the caregiver or the spouse. When a person is struggling with a mental health issue, it becomes pretty obvious that they need help, and you want to help them, but it's not always so obvious that the caregiver needs help also. So, remember when you're caring for anyone with a mental health issue as a pastor or counselor, you may see that person once or twice a week, but there's probably somebody who is going home to that person every single day. And that is daunting, so don't neglect the caregiver. Find a way to support them too. Find a way to spend individual time with that person, not just bringing them into counseling sessions with the other person. Spend some individual time with them and help them find the balance between caring for themselves and caring for the person they love. And always help them recognize the presence of Jesus.

God Is Strong When We Are Weak

In the Bible, Paul was overwhelmed with trials that affected his mental health. "We do not want you to be uninformed, brothers and sisters, about the troubles we experienced…We were under great pressure, far beyond our ability to endure, so that we despaired of life itself" (2 Corinthians 1:8 NIV). However, Paul learned that when he was weak, God's grace was sufficient to give him strength. "Not that we are competent in ourselves to claim anything for ourselves, but our competence comes from God" (3:5 NIV).

PRAYER

God, I trust that you have a plan for my suffering.
Please reveal your plan in your time.

God, I trust that your plan includes the help of others
when I need it. Please help me see your workers in my life.

God, I trust that your word will help me. Please show me
words in Scripture that will bring me comfort.

Amen.

Day 28

GRIEVING FOR MENTAL HEALTH

Life for young Justin was a rollercoaster. Some days he would be very happy, while others, he was unhappy and depressed. He had no idea why this would happen. He grew up in a good family. They were a Christian family. Justin had grown up in the church, and he knew Christ since he was a little child.

Things started to change for Justin in the first grade. He began experiencing mental health issues and depression. Headaches and stomach pain were a common occurrence. Justin was too young to even realize something was wrong with him; this was just how life was for him, it seemed. He first experienced suicidal ideations in the third grade. Death was on his mind constantly, *at the age of eight.* These thoughts and ideas would carry on all the way through high school and beyond.

Pain, in general, became a natural way of life for Justin. The depression grew worse, and at the age of nineteen, doctors finally diagnosed him with bipolar disorder. It was so severe that he had delusions in which he couldn't tell the difference between what was real and unreal. For example, he believed he had another persona who went by the name "John," who was a demon hunter. As "John," he believed he would zoom around with magical powers, killing demons. These delusions really put people in his life at a distance. He lost relationships and friendships. They were either too afraid and uncomfortable to be around him, or they just didn't know how to help.

This made college very difficult for Justin. He would attend for a couple months then drop out because he would get so sick. After a while, he would go back again and then drop out again. He would be fine for a while and then fall apart. This was the same pattern he followed in the workplace. On his good days, he was a great employee, and people loved working around him. He was diligent and would get his work done on time. But when the depression took a hold of him, he would get fired from jobs, walk off a job, or just stop going without giving notice.

Loss of friends, relationships, and jobs and navigating through the church as a Christian with mental illness was too much for Justin at times. The option of suicide was a companion of his. Just knowing there was a way out of all the pain was comforting on his worst days. He came very close to going through with it several times, and one time a friend saved his life by taking him to the hospital. That was the last time he ever got that close to going through with suicide.

Finally, with the help of counselors and medical professionals, Justin learned that many of his challenges—the delusions, depression, and suicidal ideations—were caused by chemical imbalance in his body. Today, Justin recognizes that the medical treatment of his conditions and the spiritual treatment of his conditions are both required elements to maintain a healthy life.

With the help of a Christian counselor, a loving family, and a skilled medical team, Justin was able to make real progress in terms of his mental health. His counselor began to pray for him at the end of each counseling session, and over time, Justin fell more in love with God. He has begun working more steadily and has aspirations to write and publish his own book. God gave Justin a new perspective, one where he can look back and see how much better his life is now than what it was in the past.

Wise Counsel and Biblical Insight

Truth Is Medicine for Any Disease

Justin had episodes with bipolar disorder that affected his way of thinking and altered reality. No matter what we go through, we need to keep the truth of God's Word close to our hearts. Having a strong foundation in God's truth is a necessity when dealing with mental illness.

Hope Always Helps

Life for Justin was full of pain and despair, so much so that he even entertained thoughts of suicide for years. This reveals a complete loss of hope in his life. It wasn't until he received the medical care, counseling, and support he needed that he understood that he indeed *did* have hope and that God had a future planned for him despite his mental illness.

We All Can Live Life More Abundantly

"The thief comes only to steal and kill and destroy; I have come that they may have life, and have it to the full." (John 10:10 NIV).

PRAYER

Dear Lord, life is so hard right now, and I don't know how I will be able to go on. My heart is very heavy, and I am losing all hope. Please give me strength and show me that I can live life more abundantly through you. You are my strength and my provider, and I trust that you will be with me through these dark times. Amen.

FAMILY PTSD

Life was going great for Cheri. After receiving her undergraduate degree, she worked for the Billy Graham Evangelistic Association in international ministry. She went on to get her graduate degree in psychological counseling, and her vision was to be a therapist. She ended up getting married and finished her time with the Billy Graham Association so she could start a family. Cheri continued to work in ministry part-time after the birth of her two sons.

Raising her family was a priority of Cheri's, and she wanted the best for her boys. When her youngest son was two years old, he experienced a traumatic accident that resulted in injuries that demanded a good deal of medical attention. However, his parents wouldn't discover the extent of the mental trauma from the event until later. When Cheri's son was in the first grade, he started experiencing separation anxiety, and he would have panic attacks. There were times he had to be restrained because he would have violent outbursts.

His condition worsened, and by the time her son was eleven years old, Cheri was worried about her son's safety and the safety of her family. He was hospitalized several times. Cheri and her family were part of a close-knit community, and their neighbors were very involved in their lives. Her kids would spend time with other families, but the invitations declined as her youngest son also started having violent outbursts at other households. This started to cause chaos within their community, and soon the Christian school Cheri's son was attending was no longer able to accommodate his needs.

Cheri and her husband both had a history of depression and anxiety, but both of them still had trouble understanding what was going on with their son. Cheri even had a degree in counseling and could not figure it out. Were they both just bad parents? Were they doing something wrong?

After a number of hospitalizations and testing, her son was diagnosed with PTSD stemming from the terrible accident he had at age two. The diagnosis was not a real relief for her family. She knew this was going to be a long road ahead. Her son would start taking many medications, and they would have negative effects on him. Violent behavior started between her two sons. Sometimes Cheri didn't know which child to protect and which one to manage. The mistrust that grew between the two brothers would last for years.

Seeing her child have strong emotions but not be able to communicate them was heartbreaking for Cheri. Her family was forced to isolate themselves from him at times, and that made her feel like a bad parent. The situation just seemed hopeless and too much to handle. She felt incapable of helping him, and that brought many tears. She would beat herself up with accusations like, *I should be able to handle my child. I should be able to understand my child.* These thoughts rolled around in her head and caused her to fall into her own depression. The stigma that came along with her child having a mental illness did not help matters.

However, as the years went by, God provided Cheri with a very important discovery: her son was created in the image of God and deserved to be treated with dignity, with honor, and as a special person who has something to contribute to the community. Her family had always been involved with church, and despite some of the hardships that tried to interfere with that, they continued to attend whenever they could. When Cheri's son became a teenager, God put a youth pastor in their lives who would accept and love her son no matter what. When her son attended church youth group, the youth pastor always allowed him to take breaks or leave service early in case it became too overwhelming for him. The youth pastor never criticized him or treated him differently.

One evening at youth group, Cheri's son decided he wanted to share his testimony to the other kids. He shared his struggle with depression and anxiety. The youth leader chose to let him talk, his raw emotions unedited and uncensored. His testimony was so powerful that several other kids were able to say they struggled with the same thing. Cheri now understood that her son had unique gifts and traits that reflect the image of God. Her son could still make a difference for the kingdom regardless of his mental illness.

Wise Counsel and Biblical Insight

We Must Give God Our Trauma

Therapist Trisha Vogelsang says, as humans, we become vulnerable to all the things that are in the supernatural realm, good or bad, whether that is a spirit of trauma or a spirit of rage or a spirit of isolation. "We get to experience inner healing, and we get to invite Jesus into the healing process of those shattered pieces. He puts us back together," Trisha said. "He binds up the brokenhearted. He takes the shattered, broken pieces of our lives, and he puts us back together piece by piece."

God Is in Our Families No Matter What Happens

Cheri never expected the trials and sufferings that would come from her son's mental illness. Some days things seemed to be just too hard to deal with, and God did not seem to be in the picture. However, as Cheri would discover, God was always there and was faithful to her family. He brought emotional healing to each of them as they needed it. A mental illness is like any other illness, and God can use someone with a mental illness just the same.

God Is Strong When We Are Weak

"God is our refuge and strength, an ever-present help in trouble. Therefore we will not fear, though the earth give way and the mountains fall into the heart of the sea, though its waters roar and foam and the mountains quake with their surging" (Psalm 46:1–3 NIV).

PRAYER

Dear Lord, there is chaos going on in my life, and I don't know what to do. I don't know why these things are happening to my family, but I know you are in control. I trust that you have plans that are best for me and my family, and I pray that you reveal your love and peace to us in these times. Amen.

SHARING ATTRACTS CARE

Ryan always felt uneasy and sometimes full of anxiety as a young boy. He wasn't sure why. One day, he was deathly afraid of clowns. And as a third grader, he sat in his school counselor's office explaining his fear of nuclear war. This anxiety and fear led to depression. It all came to a head in his late teens and early twenties. Thoughts inside his head started to take hold and overwhelmed him. He experienced fatigue and exhaustion from the anxiety. He lost peace and happiness like others seemed to have, and this plummeted him even deeper into depression.

He struggled with generalized anxiety, and he was diagnosed with obsessive-compulsive disorder in his twenties. He attempted suicide twice, once when he was eighteen and another time when he was twenty. Both times were triggered by romantic breakups. His family tried to make sense of what he was going through, but even Ryan didn't understand why he felt this way. It was very difficult.

These suicide attempts were a cry for help for Ryan. He felt like he had hit rock bottom. The second suicide attempt was the dark time in his life when God got a hold of him. Ryan would never try to attempt suicide again, but mental illness still followed him into adulthood and even into his eventual ministry.

Ryan joined a church that was led by its founding pastor of thirty-five years. He had attended the church for about six years before God chose him to be the next pastor. His struggles with mental health were still right there. Only two months before Ryan became the next pastor, the church conducted a series of talks that focused on breaking down the stigma associated with mental health and the church.

Knowing that he would be a pastor with mental illness caused some fear in Ryan. *Pastors were the ones who were supposed to model health and holiness, looking more like Jesus,* Ryan thought to himself at first. Other doubts crept into his mind. What if he was experiencing this because he didn't have enough faith? Ryan finally made the decision to come out and tell his congregation the complete story regarding his mental health. Although it felt good to get that off his shoulders, he still felt some anxiety over what his church might think about it. However, the next day, he was flooded with emails from people in his church who expressed how thankful they were that he shared his story and how they felt more connected with him as a pastor.

Over time, Ryan realized that sharing even his own struggles as a pastor was okay. No matter how bad things had been before or how bad they could get in his life, he was not alone, and God's love was constant just the same.

Wise Counsel and Biblical Insight

You Are Not Alone

Therapist Julie Hull says it is common for people with mental illness to believe that they are alone in their struggle: "The lies you hear in your head tell you that you're alone and you're the only one dealing with this, you're weird, messed up, crazy. To hear other people's stories, you can feel validated and realize that you're not alone."

Share Your Story

"Our stories are a way that God uses to minister to his people, and I think in heaven we're going to be hearing people's stories like this all the time for God's glory," says Julie.

God's Grace Is Perfect in Weakness

When we are struck by severe depression or anxiety, we need to remember that it is okay to be weak at times. "'My grace is sufficient for you, for my power is made perfect in weakness.' Therefore I will boast all the more gladly about my weaknesses, so that Christ's power may rest on me" (2 Corinthians 12:9 NIV).

PRAYER

God, we live in a broken world where there is pain that can be seen and pain that is beneath the surface. Help me acknowledge the invisible pain, and show me ways to encourage others who feel they are alone in their struggle. When I am hurting, help me to be transparent so I can be open to help. Amen.

HOLDING ON THROUGH DEPRESSION

After Sheila had her third child, her life changed in a way she could never have imagined. When her newborn was only a month old, Sheila started to lose sleep at night, and her mind started to race with anxiety. It got worse and worse until she wasn't sleeping at all, and her husband took her to the doctor. She was admitted to the hospital and stayed for several days. They tried to figure out what was going on with her. It wouldn't be long until Sheila learned she had a severe case of postpartum depression. She had never experienced anything like this before, and she didn't know what lay ahead for her.

Sheila felt physically and emotionally fried. The anxiety and depression affected her everyday activities. She couldn't focus on normal daily tasks. She couldn't even use her phone. At one point she didn't sleep for ten days, and the anxiety took a tremendous toll on her body and spirit. In the depth of her suffering, there were times when Sheila started to believe that this was going to be her new reality and that she would never live a happy life again. She felt that her mind was completely gone and that she wasn't going to find a way out of this.

The only thing she could do was cling to Jesus. She prayed every day that God would take this struggle away from her family so she could be the mom he wanted her to be. Sheila's father was a pastor, and she leaned into the lessons he had planted in her life, that whatever the enemy meant for evil, God could turn into good, that her job was to trust and hold on to the hope of God's promises for her. Sheila had been taught to always put God first, so even through her depression, she tried to keep God close to her. Sheila also knew that she should trust the people God put in her life in her small group at church. When she felt unable to hold herself up, she trusted that her group would provide the strength she didn't have.

There were times when Sheila was angry with God and struggled with her faith. Again, God reached her through someone in her life. Sheila's mother assured her that it was normal to question God's presence sometimes, that sometimes it might feel like God isn't near you at all. In those times it might seem like you are just going through the motions of being faithful to him and praying to him. Even in those times of doubt, he is hearing every word, and he is going to restore you.

Gradually, God did restore Sheila's mental health to where she could experience peace again. Small improvements encouraged Sheila to cling to God's promises, promises that he had a plan for her life and plans for her to prosper. This gave her hope for the first time in a long time.

Once she had hope in her life, things really started to change. She read in her Bible that God was working out everything in her life for good, even the bad things.

With the reminder of things she had learned years earlier and with faith strengthened by her own experiences, Sheila is now applying the lessons she's learned to help other young mothers who are experiencing postpartum depression. While she was struggling with her own mental health, she learned that the smallest gesture could mean the world to someone going through depression. Sheila now tells others that God knows their hearts, and he will always be there for them no matter what.

Looking back, Sheila can see the way God had been paving the way in her life for years before her struggle with depression. God had placed people in her life who would equip her and support her in a time when she was unable to sustain herself.

Wise Counsel and Biblical Insight

Todd Mulliken

Sheila's story of her battle with postpartum depression explains so well the episodic nature of depression. Sheila's grounding in her dependency on Jesus, her willingness to listen to wise loved ones in her life who didn't try to fix her but instead walked alongside her, and her wisdom to know that she now can walk alongside others who struggle with postpartum depression is a testimony to God's love and power to restore the broken and vulnerable.

God Will Provide Peace in Troubled Times: Suggested Scripture from Pastor Paul Johnson

"Peace I leave with you; my peace I give you. I do not give to you as the world gives. Do not let your hearts be troubled and do not be afraid" (John 14:27 NIV).

God Is Our Hope in Every Trial: Suggested Scripture from Pastor Paul Johnson

"We are hard pressed on every side, but not crushed; perplexed, but not in despair; persecuted, but not abandoned; struck down, but not destroyed" (2 Corinthians 4:8–9 NIV).

PRAYER

Dear Lord, living in this broken world is exhausting. It can be discouraging when I am tired or when circumstances just won't change for the better. As my pain has continued, I've come to realize that I have nothing left to give. Now I turn to you for help. Be the strength that has left me. Be the strong tower that never waivers or falls. Be the rock of salvation that you've promised to be. I desperately need your peace, your hope, and your love. Amen.

About the Authors

Jon Watje is a native of Minneapolis, Minnesota. He received a bachelor's degree in mass communication and journalism from Oklahoma Christian University. He worked as a journalist in Oklahoma City where he became an editor of two newspapers for ten years. Jon's work received awards from the Oklahoma Press Association for news writing, feature writing, and photography. Jon moved back to the Minneapolis area where he now lives with his wife and son. He joined Five Stone Media in 2019 and enjoys writing stories about people who have overcome trauma and grief.

Lee Bailey-Seiler serves as the operations director for Five Stone Media and Chief Curriculum Developer for LifeSupport. Having experienced transformation from addiction through Christ-centered recovery ministry, Lee knows firsthand that hopelessness is overcome when survivors share their stories of struggle and redemption. Lee and his wife live in Minnesota and have four grown children and four grandchildren.

Steve Johnson serves as the executive director and cofounder of Five Stone Media. Steve is an Emmy-Award winning producer who left the broadcast world in order to dedicate his time to the work of Five Stone Media. Steve produced live and taped events for ESPN, FOX Networks, Turner Broadcasting, and others. Steve had the honor of interviewing many of the survivors featured in this book.

Contributors

Tom Colbert, Therapist: Days 1, 11

Kim DeBerge, Therapist: Day 14

Allie Dietert, Therapist: Days 7, 13

Terri Hands, Licensed Marriage and Family Therapist (retired): Days 13, 22

Julie Hull, Licensed Pastoral Counselor and Leadership Coach: Days 12, 30

Paul Johnson, Senior Pastor: Days 2, 3, 4, 8, 9, 10, 12, 16, 19, 31

Pam Lanhart, Recovery Coach: Day 15

Todd Mulliken, MS, Licensed Professional Clinical Counselor: Days 16, 19, 31

Dan Munson, Licensed Professional Counselor and Pastor: Day 24

Jenita Pace, Licensed Professional Counselor: Days 21, 23, 25

Tim Pace, Pastor: Day 27

Jessica Teresi, Advocate for Sexual Abuse Survivors: Days 5, 6, 17, 18

Trisha Vogelsang, Licensed Marriage and Family Therapist: Days 26, 29